Essential Series

Springer

London
Berlin
Heidelberg
New York
Barcelona
Budapest
Hong Kong
Milan
Paris
Santa Clara
Singapore
Tokyo

John Cowell

Essential Delphi 3 *fast*

Includes ActiveX Development

With 179 figures

Springer

Author and Series Editor

John Cowell, BSc (Hons), MPhil, PhD
Department of Computer and Information Sciences
De Montfort University, Kents Hill Campus,
Hammerwood Gate, Kents Hill, Milton Keynes, MK7 6HP, UK

|| 559535

ISBN 3-540-76150-0 Springer-Verlag Berlin Heidelberg New York

British Library Cataloguing in Publication Data
Cowell, John, 1957-
   Essential Delphi 3.0 fast : includes ActiveX control development
   1.Delphi   (Computer program language)
   I.Title II.Delphi 3.0 fast
   005.2'62
   ISBN 3540761500

Library of Congress Cataloging-in-Publication Data
Cowell, John, 1957-
   Essential Delphi 3.0 fast : ;includes ActiveX control development /
John Cowell.
      p.   cm. - -   (Essential series)
   Includes index.
   ISBN 3-540-76150-0 (pbk. : alk. paper)
   1. Computer software- -Development.   2. Delphi (Computer file)
I. Title.   II. Series: Essential series (springer-Verlag)
QA76.76.D47C68   1997   97-40559
005.26'8- -dc21   CIP

© Springer-Verlag London Limited 1998
Printed in Great Britain

Typesetting: Camera ready by author
Printed and bound at the Athenæum Press Ltd., Gateshead, Tyne and Wear
34/3830-543210 Printed on acid-free paper

Contents

1

Why Use Delphi 3?

Introduction

Delphi has sold half a million copies world wide and is the preferred integrated development environment (IDE) for many professional programmers. If you are serious about developing applications for a Windows 95 environment Delphi is one of the best choices. The other main integrated development environments that you should consider are Visual Basic, Visual C++ and C++ Builder. Visual Basic is not an object oriented environment and while Visual C++ and C++ Builder are both excellent products, many developers prefer to use Delphi which offers a serious object oriented environment and encourages a more structured approach to application writing than C++.

Many professional programmers prefer Delphi to any other IDE. It has a great user interface, a more extensive set of tools than any other IDE, and produces efficient applications which run fast.

Version 3 is a significant improvement over version 2. Virtually any application you want to write for a Windows 95 environment can be created with Delphi. In particular version 3 now supports ActiveX and Active Form development which allows you to create your own re-usable controls and interactive Web applications.

When an IDE is as powerful as Delphi, it can be intimidating for a new programmer, but Delphi is a very well designed product and while Delphi does have very many facilities, it is organised in a logical way which makes it easier to learn. The Delphi user interface is one of the best IDEs ever. Initially Delphi may seem complicated but most users find that within a few days they can write applications and become fairly proficient within a month. Existing visual programmers will enjoy using the powerful Delphi IDE and those new to this type of environment will find it an excellent product to learn.

What this book covers

The background programming language for Delphi is Object Pascal. This book assumes that you have no prior knowledge of either Delphi, or Pascal, however it does assume that you have had some experience of programming in a high level language. Even if you have used Pascal it is worthwhile looking at the chapters which deal with the Object Pascal language, especially if your skills are a bit rusty and you need to refresh them, or if you have used a different Pascal dialect from the Borland variety. This book is also suitable for those at an intermediate level who want to learn how to develop serious, professional applications. It is assumed that you have some experience of using Windows 95 programs such as word processors, spreadsheets and databases.

When learning Delphi it is helpful if you already have some programming experience, but all the essential elements of the Delphi Pascal language are covered. If you have used Pascal or 'C' before, you will be able to switch to Delphi without any problems.

Delphi is a new language produced by Borland to challenge the highly successful Visual Basic development environment produced by Microsoft, and although the manuals supplied are fairly comprehensive, they are not error free. The on-line Help is good - the sort of standard that you have come to expect from a major company such as Borland. These are fine if you have a good grasp of Delphi and need to look up a specific point. The manuals and Help are not very good at providing a readable, impartial guide to the language and environment. This book does not cover every minor detail of Delphi in the same way as the manuals, but it does give you a grasp of all the most important features of the language. There are many illustrations and examples. The best way to learn Delphi is to try out the examples for yourself.

Getting started

When you are learning a new IDE you will need to practice a lot. This book has many examples and you should try them if possible. There are many pictures showing each stage of creating these applications and ideally you should read the book while working at your computer.

You can either use this book as a guide starting at the beginning and working through to the end, or just look at individual chapters if you already have some experience of Delphi.

This book is not intended to be a definitive in-depth description of Delphi - if it did it would be about ten times as long and take twenty times as long to read. The philosophy of this book is to cover the key features of Delphi, with many examples and diagrams. Most people find that at first they do not need to learn everything about the language to be able to develop useful programs. If, for example, your first Delphi program does not use databases, you do not need to read the chapter on databases in order to start. The best way to use this book is to read the sections you need and to try the examples. One of the pleasures of Delphi is that it allows you to develop applications *fast* - you do not even need to read all of this book before you can start!

What computer you need to run Delphi 3

Computers are never fast enough and rarely have enough disk space or memory, so the faster and more powerful your computer the better. Realistically though, Delphi can be run with quite a modest configuration and still provide reasonable performance.

The minimum configuration for reasonable performance is:

- 80486dx4.
- 16Mb of memory.

Delphi runs successfully on the minimum configuration; however, it does not run fast unless you have a higher specification computer.

The current standard for serious professional developers is:

- Pentium 200.
- 64Mb of memory.

There are great improvements in performance using a Pentium processor with 32Mb or more of memory, but a dx4 processor with 32Mb of memory is likely to run Delphi faster than a Pentium processor with 16Mb of memory.

The standard monitor size has now increased from 14" to 15", but even if you have excellent eyesight a 17" monitor is a substantial improvement.

If you want to run Delphi at the same time as other Windows software you should have even more memory than this in order to reduce the amount of swapping between disk and memory which is much slower than referring to memory alone. The minimum amount of disk space is 40Mb, but a full implementation needs 80Mb.

Although these system requirements may seem high, they are typical of the computer needed to use any of the popular IDEs.

What's new in Delphi 3

If you are not an experienced programmer and are not switching from version 2 to version 3 of Delphi you can skip this section. If you have used Delphi 2 applications there are some significant changes that you should be aware of. The main changes are:

- Code insight. This is a most helpful enhancement which displays context sensitive help when you are typing Object Pascal code.
- Component templates. Delphi allows you to create a set of components and to add them to a form in one step.
- Additional visual components. Many new visual components have been added, for all aspects of application design, including database and ActiveX/COM components.
- Run-time library enhancements. These changes are very limited, the principal changes are three new functions **SumInt**, **MinInt** and **MaxInt** for returning the sum, minimum and maximum of an array of integers.

- Compiler changes. Package, OLE and ActiveX objects support is provided. Assertions are supported to test for conditions that must be met if the application has not encountered an error. A compiler directive allows assertions to be switched on or off. The True Boolean data type **ByteBool**, **WordBool** and **LongBool** are represented by –1 for compatibility with Visual Basic. The Boolean data type continues to represent True as 1 and False as 0.
- Multi-byte character support. Numerous functions have been changed or added to support multi-byte characters.
- New BDE and SQL links. Version 4.0 of the Borland Database Engine and SQL Links is included.
- COM support and ActiveX creation. Wizards are available to allow you to create ActiveX controls.
- Creation and support of Active Forms.
- Package support. Packages are dynamic-link libraries (DLLs) which allow applications to share code. The Delphi Visual Component Library itself is split into packages. The most commonly used components are in a package called VCL30.DPL. You only need one copy of this and other packages however many applications you run.
- IDE enhancements. There are numerous IDE enhancements. The most important are: version information can be included in your application; unit files can be stored in different directories to the rest of your application; a shared repository directory can be specified.

Converting from Delphi 2 to Delphi 3

Most applications written under version 2 should run without problems under version 3, however there are a few changes which are discussed at length in the Delphi Help. To see these changes click on the **Help** menu, select the **Index** page and search for **Compatibility with version 2**. This is an exhaustive list of the changes.

Conventions

There are a few conventions used in this book which make it easier to read:

- All program examples are in *italics.*
- All reserved words such as **begin...end** are in **Bold**.
- All user defined names such as *MyFile* are in *italics*.
- All Delphi default names such as *Edit1* are in *italics*
- Menu options such as the **File | Close** which means the **Close** option from the **File** menu are in **Bold.**

Non-American English speakers need to be aware of the American spellings of reserved words such as color and dialog if time consuming errors are to be minimised.

2
The Delphi Environment

Introduction

The Delphi environment is a serious development environment which is widely used by computing professionals throughout the world. One of the drawbacks if you are new to programming in Delphi is that you have to understand a large and complex environment in order to use all of the facilities that Delphi offers. On the positive side, Delphi is very logically organised and you can ignore many aspects of the environment if you do not want to use them. If you are not used to other visual programming environments such as Visual Basic, Visual C++, or one of the Java environments, Delphi will seem complicated at first, but it is regarded by professionals as one of the best environments available. You will quickly find that you can develop your own applications. The aim of this chapter is to introduce you to the essential elements of the environments.

In this chapter you will learn about:

- Running Delphi.
- Creating a shortcut to Delphi.
- The main features of the Delphi development environment.

Running Delphi

You can run Delphi from the Windows 95 taskbar as shown in fig 2.1:

- Click on **Start** on the taskbar.
- Select the **Programs** option.
- Select the **Borland Delphi** 3 option.
- Select the **Delphi 3** option.

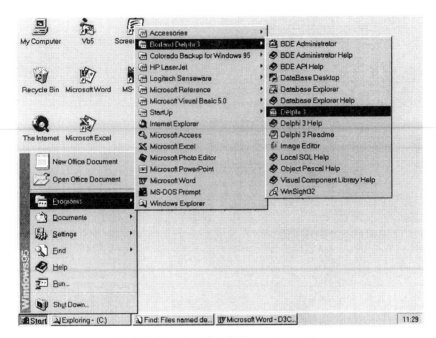

Fig 2.1 Running Delphi from the taskbar.

It is likely that you will be running Delphi a lot, so it makes sense to create a shortcut, so that you can run it by clicking on an icon on your desktop.

The first stage in creating a shortcut is to run the Windows Explorer. The Delphi file you need to create the shortcut to is called Delphi32.exe. If you have installed Delphi using the default folder structure it will be in a folder called C:\Program Files\Borland\Delphi32\BIN. If you cannot find this file:

- Select the **Find | Tools** option from the Explorer menu.
- Specify in the **Named** text box that the file you are searching for is Delphi32.exe.
- Set the **Look In** text box to the name of the drive where the file is stored, this will be C: for most systems.
- Check the **Include subfolders** check box.
- Click on **Find Now**.

The window shown in fig 2.2 is displayed.

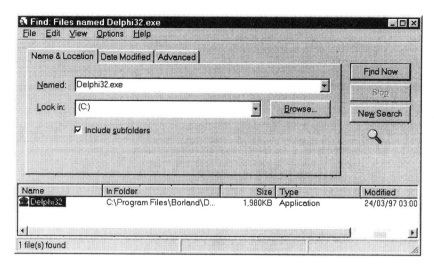

Fig 2.2 *Searching for Delphi.*

To create the shortcut right click on the Delphi32 icon (not on the folder name) and select the **Create Shortcut** menu option. A warning dialog box shown in fig 2.3 will be displayed. If you have not done this before, this is the point at which it seems that you have made a mistake, but this is not the case if you see this dialog box.

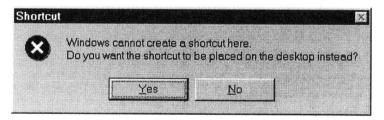

Fig 2.3 *Creating a shortcut to Delphi.*

Click on **Yes**. When you have closed Explorer and returned to your desktop you will see an icon called **Shortcut to Delphi32**. You can rename this by right clicking on it and selecting the **Rename** option.

The Delphi Environment

When Delphi runs, the design environment will be similar to the one shown in fig 2.4. Your screen may look a little different since it is straightforward to resize all of the windows and to choose which parts of the environment are displayed.

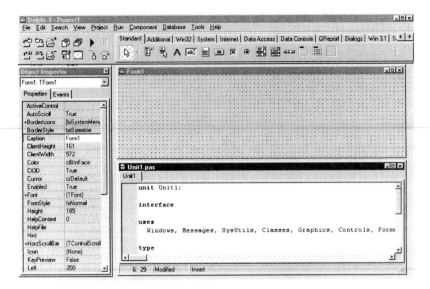

Fig 2.4 *The Delphi environment.*

The key parts of the environment are:

- The design form.
- The Component Palette.
- The Object Inspector.
- The unit window.
- The menu.
- The SpeedBar.

In the next section we are going to look at each of these elements in turn.

The design form

Virtually all the applications that you will write will have at least one form. When you first run Delphi or when you start creating a new application, Delphi automatically creates a single form for you. You can create as many other forms both at design time and run-time as you want. The design form shown in fig 2.5 is a standard Windows 95 form. The window can be maximised, minimised or closed in the usual way. It can also be resized by dragging on the border. The only unusual feature of this form is that it is covered in a matrix of dots. This grid is useful when you are designing your applications. Any component placed on the form will snap so that the top left corner is positioned on one these grid points. You can adjust the spacing of the grid points or turn off the snap facility, but the default Delphi settings work well for most applications.

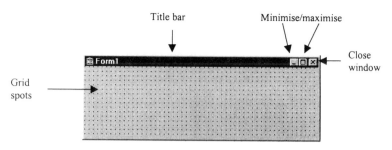

Fig 2.5 The design form.

The title bar contains the form **Caption**, this is a property of the form that can be easily changed using the Object Inspector.

The Component Palette

Windows applications make use of a wide range of components, such as labels, text boxes and lists. The Component Palette has an extensive range of components which you can use to create your applications. There are also many thousands of components from software companies which you can add. If you want a special component which is not available elsewhere, you can even create your own. There are 12 pages in the component palette in the professional version and an additional page called Decision Cube in the Client/Server version. The Standard page is shown in fig 2.6

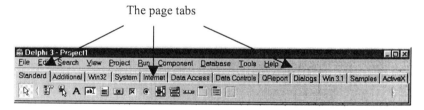

Fig 2.6 The Standard Component Palette.

Each of the icons shown represents a different component. If you want to display and use a different set of components click on one of the page tabs.

When you want to add a component to a form:

- Click on the component you want on the Component Palette.
- Move the mouse to the form in roughly the position that you want the component to go.
- Drag the mouse. The position where you first press the left button to start dragging will become the top left or the bottom right of the component.
- You can resize the component by dragging on one of the sizing handles as shown in fig 2.7.

Sizing handles

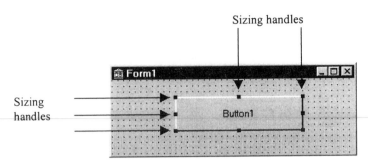

Fig 2.7 Resizing a component.

You can move the component by clicking on the component (not on one of the sizing handles) to select it and dragging.

The Object Inspector

All of the components and other objects such as the design form have a set of properties, for example, a form has a property called **Caption**, which is the text which appears at the top of the form. Visual components such as buttons also have a set of events associated with them. These are events which can occur in a Windows 95 application which the component can respond to. A button has an **OnClick** event and you can write Object Pascal code which will take some action when a button is clicked, that is when the **OnClick** event for button component occurs.

When you select an object, the Object Inspector displays the properties and events of that object.

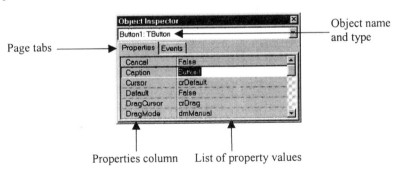

Fig 2.8 The Object Inspector.

The Object Inspector has two tabs, one shows the properties of the selected object and the other the events. If you put more than one component on a form and select each one in turn you will see that the properties and their values in the Object Inspector change.

The unit window

The unit window is where you can view and edit the Object Pascal code in your project. Every time you create a new form you create a new unit file. You can switch between the units by clicking on the page tabs as shown in fig 2.9.

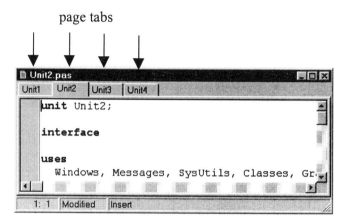

Fig 2.9 Viewing and editing unit files.

Delphi has a powerful editor, including all of the facilities that you would expect such as search and replace and cut and paste. When an event such as a button click occurs you can write some code in the unit file associated with the form containing the button which will take the required action. You will see how to do this in the next chapter.

Every form has a unit file, in addition you can create object Pascal files which do not have a form associated with them. These are viewed and amended in the same way as the unit files.

The menu

The menu bar shown in fig 2.10 has ten entries, each of which has many items.

Fig 2.10 The Delphi menu.

We will be looking at most of these options throughout this book, but the Delphi on-line help is particularly good in this area. If you want to find out in detail what a menu item does, select the item and press **F1**. This will invoke the context sensitive help.

The SpeedBar

The SpeedBar shown in fig 2.11 provides a shortcut way of using some of the most common menu items.

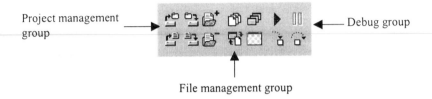

Project management group →   ← Debug group

File management group

Fig 2.11 The SpeedBar.

The default SpeedBar has three groups of buttons, but you can delete and add new buttons to the SpeedBar if you find that you are frequently using a particular menu option.

Finding windows

One of the most frustrating things about using a new development environment, particularly one as powerful as Delphi is that it is easy to lose a window, either by closing it or by simply covering it with another window. Fortunately, the **View** menu helps you to find lost objects.

*Table 2.1 The **View** menu.*

Object	Menu Option	Shortcut key
Object Inspector.	**View	Object Inspector**	**F11**
Forms.	**View	Forms**	**Shift+F12**
Component Palette.	**View	Component Palette**	None.
Units.	**View	Units**	**Ctrl+F12**
Switch between a form and its unit file.	**View |Toggle Form/Unit**	**F12**
SpeedBar.	**View	SpeedBar**	None.

The best way to become familiar with a new development environment is to use it to create a new application. We are going to do this in the next chapter.

3

The Standard Component Palette

Introduction

The Component Palette has 12 pages in the Professional version and 13 in the Client/Server version which contain virtually all of the components you need for creating Windows applications. The most commonly used group of components are on the Standard page. In this chapter you will learn:

- What event driven software is.
- What components are.
- How to change component properties.
- How the components on the Standard page behave.

Event Driven Software

Windows applications use forms which contain a variety of components (or controls in Visual Basic jargon). Every component and form has a series of events that it can respond to, for example, when you click on a button an **OnClick** event occurs for that button. Delphi automatically creates an outline procedure for each event that can occur. You can add your own code to this event handler which will take some action in response to the button click. If a form contains more than one button, each button has its own event handler, so that different things can happen in response to different buttons being clicked. Every component and form can respond to many different events. This is the basis of all Windows programming and you will see many examples of it throughout this book.

Every component and form also has its own set of properties, for example a form has a **Caption** property, which is the text which appears at the top of the form.

In this chapter we are going to look at the components on the Standard Component Palette and the key properties and events of these components.

Changing component properties

You can change the properties of a component at design time and also at run-time. In this section we are going to look at how to change properties at design time.

To change a property you need to select the component whose properties you want to change. You can do this by clicking on the component. The Object Inspector will display the properties and events of the selected component. If you cannot see the Object Inspector, press **F11** or choose the **View | Object Inspector** menu option. Make sure that the Properties page is selected by clicking on that page tab.

There are three types of properties that you can change.

- The first sort requires you to select and type the value of the new property. The **Caption** property shown in fig 3.1 belongs to this group.

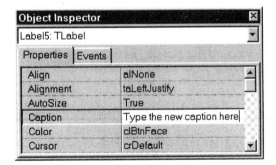

*Fig 3.1 Changing the **Caption** property*

- Many properties offer you a choice of property values, for example the **AutoSize** property which can be either True or False. These are indicated by a down pointing arrow on the left of the property as shown in fig 3.2.

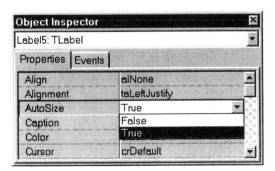

*Fig 3.2 Changing the **Caption** property.*

- The final type opens a dialog box which allows you to select a range of options. The **Font** property falls into this category. It has a small '+' sign on the far left. When you double click on this a series of properties are displayed. One of these sub-properties **Style** also has a '+' sign adjacent to it as shown in fig 3.3 and can be expanded further.

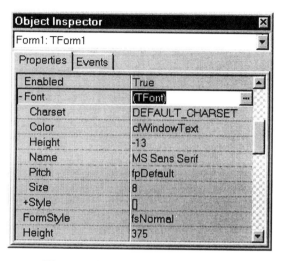

*Fig 3.3 Changing the **Font** property.*

The **Font** property also has 3 dots on the far left, which indicates that a dialog box will appear if clicked. The dialog box in this case is shown in fig 3.4.

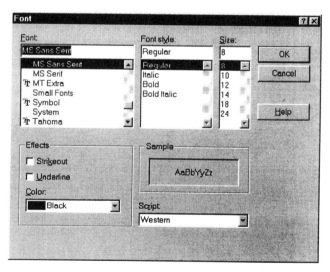

Fig 3.4 The Font dialog.

Many of the properties in this dialog are also accessible by clicking on the '+' sign adjacent to the **Font** property.

The Label component

The **Label** component is used to display text that the application user cannot change. The icon for this component is shown in fig 3.5.

*Fig 3.5 The **Label** icon.*

This is the most simple of the components available, but there are still some important properties that you can control to alter its appearance as shown in fig 3.6.

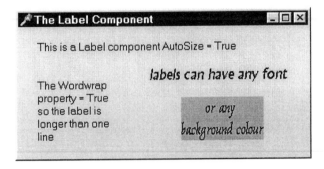

Fig 3.6 Examples of the Label component.

- If the **AutoSize** property is set to True, the label will automatically change so that it is just big enough to fit the text.
- If the **WordWrap** property is True, the label can be more than one line long.
- The **Alignment** property determines whether the text is centred, left aligned or right aligned.
- Two important properties that labels share with many other components are **Color** and **Font**. The **Color** property is the background of the label. The **Font** property also has a **Color** sub-property which is the colour of the font.
- A useful property of labels is that you can ensure that other components are not obscured by setting the **Transparent** property to true.

The first label to be created is called *Label1*, the second is *Label2* and so on.

The Edit component

The **Edit** component shown in fig 3.7 is used to display or read a single line of text.

*Fig 3.7 The **Edit** component.*

The text which is displayed is stored in the **Text** property. The main limitation of the **Edit** component compared to the **Memo** component is that you can only have one line of text. Unlike the **Label** component you can type or edit text at run-time. Two examples are shown in fig 3.8.

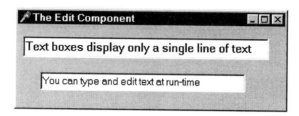

*Fig 3.8 Examples of the **Edit** component.*

In common with most other components you can control the **Font**, **Color** and **Alignment** properties.

One important property of **Edit** components is that you can prevent text being displayed on the screen as it is typed if, for example, you are typing a password. This is done by setting the **PasswordChar** property of the component to a single letter, which is echoed every time any printable key is pressed.

A useful property is **Modified**, which is set to True if the contents of the component are changed. The first **Edit** component is called *Edit1*.

The Memo component

The **Memo** component shown in fig 3.9 is used to display or read many lines of text. You can control the maximum amount of text by setting the **MaxLength** property to the number of characters. When you input text and reach the maximum no further input is accepted. If **MaxLength** is set to zero, there is no limit on the amount of text. In practice, however there are problems when more than 255K of text is entered.

*Fig 3.9 The **Memo** component.*

You can add scroll bars to a memo by setting the **ScrollBars** property to display vertical, horizontal scroll bars or both. Two examples are shown in fig 3.10.

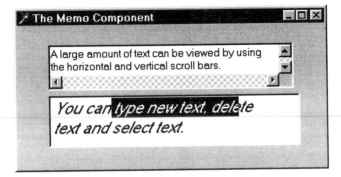

Fig 3.10 Examples of the Memo component.

Text can be added to a memo by setting the **Lines** property. Double click on this property to display the String list editor as shown in fig 3.11.

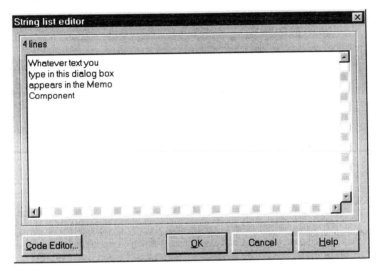

Fig 3.11 The String list editor.

You can select text. The **SelStart** property gives the starting position of the selected text. **SelLength** gives the length. **SelText** is a string containing the selected text. The first memo created is called *Memo1*.

The Button component

Buttons have a single line of centred text as shown in fig 3.13. This is the **Caption** property. Buttons are used to initiate some action. When you click on a button an **OnClick** event occurs. You put the code that carries out the actions you want in the **OnClick** event handler for the button. You will see how to do this in the next chapter.

*Fig 3.12 The **Button** component.*

The simple button as shown in fig 3.13 is still the most widely used of the button components in Windows applications. The **BitBtn** component behaves in a similar way, but allows you to put a graphical image on the face of the button.

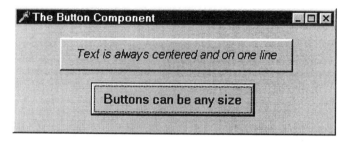

*Fig 3.13 Examples of the **Button** component.*

The CheckBox component

The **CheckBox** component shown in fig 3.14 is used to indicate if an option is True or False. Checkboxes are usually logically grouped together, but apart from this, there is no actual connection between them, unlike radio buttons as you will see shortly.

*Fig 3.14 The **Checkbox** component.*

The text displayed alongside the checkbox is in the **Caption** property. You can place the text on the right or left of the checkbox itself by setting the **Alignment** property as shown in fig 3.15.

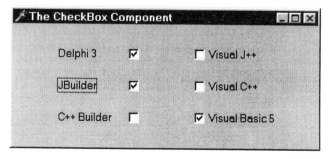

*Fig 3.15 Examples of the **CheckBox** component.*

When a check box has a small tick, the **Checked** property is True. If you do not want an option to be available at run-time set the **Enabled** property to False. This will grey the checkbox and its text.

The RadioButton component

The **RadioButton** component, shown in fig 3.16, is similar to the **CheckBox** component in that it is used to indicate a True or False option.

Fig 3.16 The RadioButton component.

The difference is that radio buttons are usually grouped together in either a **Panel**, **GroupBox** or **ScrollBox** component. If they are, only one of the group of **RadioButton** components can be set to true. If you do not explicitly place the components within a container component, the form itself acts as a container. When you have placed the radio buttons within a container you can select the container and move it and all the components within it as a single group.

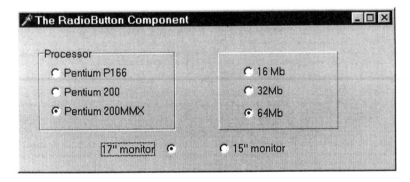

*Fig 3.17 Examples of the **RadioButton** component.*

In common with checkboxes, radio buttons can be made unavailable using the **Enabled** property, and the **Alignment** property used to place the button on the right or left of the text.

The ListBox component

The **ListBox** component, shown in fig 3.18, displays a list of options.

*Fig 3.18 The **ListBox** component.*

If the **MultiSelect** property is False (the default) you can select one item in the list as shown in fig 3.19. If it is True you can select as many items as you wish. You cannot modify or type any items at run-time, except by writing some Object Pascal code. The text displayed in a list box is a string list specified by the **Items** property. You can display items alphabetically by setting the **Sorted** property to True.

*Fig 3.19 Example of the **ListBox** component.*

You can display items in more than one column by changing the value of the **Columns** property from its default of 1.

The ComboBox component

The **ComboBox** component, shown in fig 3.20, is very similar to **ListBox** components except that the user can either select an item from a pre-defined list or type their own text.

*Fig 3.20 The **ComboBox** component.*

The **Items** property contains the text of the list in a string list. Unlike the **ListBox** component, the **ComboBox** component has a **Text** property which contains the text which is currently selected.

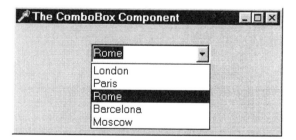

*Fig 3.21 Example of the **ComboBox** component.*

The **ComboBox** component is available in five different types. You can determine which one to use by setting the **Style** property:

Table 3.1 The **Style** property

Value	Description
csDropDown	A drop-down list with an edit box so that text can be entered at run-time.
csSimple	A fixed list with an edit box. The list length is determined by the **Height** property of the combo box.
csDropDownList	A drop-down list without an edit box, so text cannot be entered at run-time.
csOwnerDrawFixed	A drop-down list with an edit box. The space allowed for each item is determined by the **ItemHeight** property.
csOwnerDrawVariable	A drop-down list with an edit box. The space between each item is variable.

The ScrollBar component

Many components such as memos have integral scroll bars. The **ScrollBar** component, shown in fig 3.22, allows you to add scroll bars to components which do not have them. There are two types, vertical and horizontal, which are determined by the **Kind** property.

Fig 3.22 The ScrollBar component.

The position of the bar is indicated by the **Position** property. The minimum and maximum values of this property are given by the **Min** and **Max** property values.

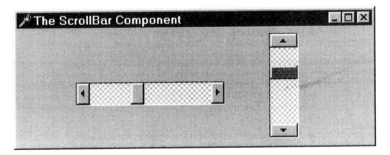

Fig 3.23 Example of the **ScrollBar** component.

There are three ways to move the bar:

• You can drag the bar itself.

- Click on either of the end arrows. The distance moved is given by the **SmallChange** property.
- Click on either side of the moveable bar. The distance moved is given by the **LargeChange** property.

The GroupBox and RadioGroup components

The **GroupBox** component, shown in fig 3.24, is used to group other components, such as radio buttons, so that they can be treated as a single group.

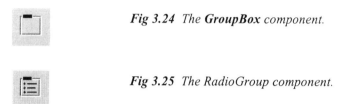

Fig 3.24 The **GroupBox** *component.*

Fig 3.25 The RadioGroup *component.*

In fig 3.26 the left group consists of a **GroupBox** component and three **RadioButton** components. The right group consists of a single **RadioGroup**. They appear exactly the same in appearance at run-time, but have to be treated differently at design time.

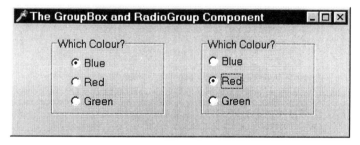

Fig 3.26 Example of the **GroupBox** and **RadioGroup** components.

The most commonly used components placed within a group box are radio buttons, so it is efficient to combine these two components together. To add radio buttons to the **RadioGroup** component, use the **Items** property. Each line typed in the String list editor becomes a radio button. The **ItemIndex** property indicates which radio button has been selected. The radio button at the top of the list has an index of 0 and so on. A value of −1 indicates that no button is selected.

The Panel component

The **Panel** component, shown in fig 3.27 is a container component.

*Fig 3.27 The **Panel** component.*

The main use for this component is that it can have a variety of bevelled edges, which may improve the appearance of a form. A few examples are shown in fig 3.28.

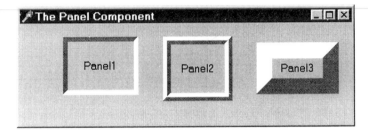

*Fig 3.28 Examples of the **Panel** component.*

The properties which control the bevelling are:

- **BevelInner** and **BevelOuter**. These properties can have the value **bvLowered, bvRaised** or **bvNone**.
- **BevelWidth**. The width of the bevel.

MainMenu and PopupMenu

Delphi allows you to create both main menus which appear as a menu bar at the top of a form and popup menus which appear in response to a right mouse button click. This is an important area and is covered in detail in chapter 13.

Using the components

This chapter has looked at some of the most commonly used components, but the best way to learn about the components is to use them. The next chapter looks at writing the user interface side of an application.

4

Using the Standard Components

Introduction

In the previous chapter you saw the components on the Standard Component Palette. This chapter creates an application using most of those components, so that you can see how they interact together. The best way to learn Delphi is to create this application for yourself and to try a few variations. Some Object code is needed to make this application work correctly. If you are not familiar with programming in this language, do not worry, it is covered in detail later in this book. If you do have some previous programming experience you should be able to follow the code.

In this chapter you will learn about:

- Adding components to forms.
- Changing component properties at run-time.
- Using event procedures.
- Compiling and linking programs.
- Running programs.

The Changeling application

This application displays some text in a memo box and allows you to change many of its properties, including the font, the text size and the foreground and background colours. The completed working application is shown in fig 4.1.

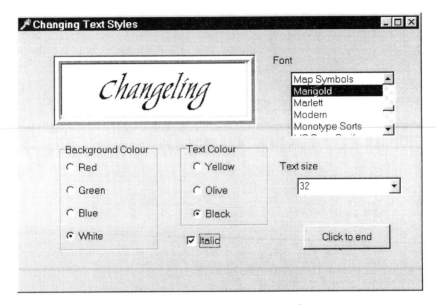

Fig 4.1 The running Changeling application.

The following components are used:

- A **RadioGroup** component is used to specify the background colour, while the text colour is changed by a **GroupBox** component with three **RadioButton** components.
- A **ListBox** component is used to change the font and a drop down **ComboBox** component to control the size.
- A **CheckBox** component determines whether the text is italic or not.
- The text itself is typed into a **Memo** component which is surrounded by a **Panel** component to provide it with a border.

Creating the user interface

One of the great advantages of Delphi over non-visual programming environments is that it is straightforward to create your user interface, so your applications have a serious professional feel. If you decide that you do not like the appearance of your form you can easily change it.

The first step is to create a new folder on your computer where you can save this application. It is standard practice to put every new application into a separate folder. If you do not do this and use the default names for files when you save the project, files will be overwritten. The easiest way to create a new folder is to use the Windows Explorer and the **File | New | Folder** option.

When you run Delphi it automatically starts a new application, however if you have an existing application open in Delphi you need to start a new application by selecting the **File | New Application** menu option.

Adding the Memo and Panel components

To add the components:

- Select the Standard page of the Component Palette.
- Select the Panel icon on the palette and place a **Panel** component on the form. Adjust it to the size you want.
- Set the **BevelWidth** property to 5.
- Set the **BevelInner** property to **bvLowered**.
- Set the **BevelOuter** property to **bvRaised**.
- Add a **Memo** component to the form so that it is on top of the panel. Adjust it so that it fits neatly within the panel.
- Change the text in the memo by selecting the **Lines** property and typing the text you want to be displayed in the String list editor.

You must add the memo to the panel, not the other way around, otherwise the panel will not be visible. Since the panel acts as a container for the memo, if you select the panel and move it, the memo will move with it.

Adding the ListBox and ComboBox components

- Select the **ListBox** component and add it to the form.
- Add a **Label** component just above the list box and change its **Caption** property to *Font*.
- Add the **ComboBox** component to the form.
- Change its **Text** property so that it is blank.
- In this application we are using the default **Style** property of **csDropDown**, so this property will not have to be changed.

Adding the RadioButtons

To add the two sets of radio buttons:

- Select the **RadioGroup** component and add it to the form.
- Click on the small button with 3 dots on the right of the **Items** property.
- Add the text *Red Green Blue White* on successive lines in the String list editor.
- Change the **Caption** property of the **RadioGroup** component to *Background Colour*.

The second group of radio buttons are within a **GroupBox** component.

- Add the **GroupBox** component to the form.
- Change its **Caption** property to *Text colour*.
- Add three **RadioButton** components to the **GroupBox** component.

• Change the **Caption** properties of these radio buttons to Yellow, Olive and Black.

Completing the user interface

To complete the form add a button and a **CheckBox** component. Change the button's **Caption** property to *Click to end*, and the check box's **Caption** property to *Italic*.

The form you have created should look similar to the form below. If any component is not the correct size, or is not in an ideal position, select it and change it.

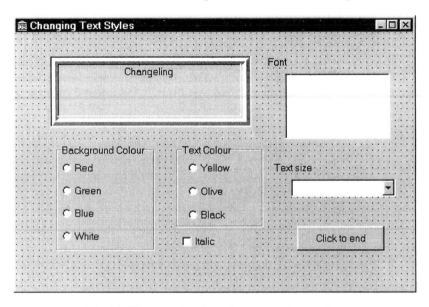

Fig 4.2 The completed application at design time.

The user interface is complete and you can run this application by clicking on the **Run** icon on the toolbar as shown in fig 4.3.

The **Run** icon    *Fig 4.3 The Run icon.*

You can also run the application by choosing the **Run** | **Run** menu option or by pressing **F9**.

The application does run, the form can be moved, resized, minimised and maximised, but nothing works. In order to add some functionality to the application some Object Pascal must be written. Do not worry if you are not an experienced programmer and do not understand all aspects of the next section. Object Pascal is covered in detail later in this book.

Changing the text colour

Only one of the three buttons for changing the text colour can be selected at any time. If you select one radio button the others within the group box are deselected. Whenever you change the state of a radio button, an **OnClick** event occurs. You need to add some code to that change event. Delphi creates an outline procedure for you. To find this procedure:

- Select the top radio button, which has the caption *Yellow.*
- Select the Events page of the Object Inspector.
- Double click on the column on the right of the **OnClick** event.
- The code window is displayed as shown in fig 4.4.

Fig 4.4 The Object Inspector and the Code window.

The outline procedure is shown below:

> ***procedure*** *TForm1.RadioButton1Click(Sender: TObject);*
> ***begin***
>
> ***end;***

The procedure name *TForm1.RadioButton1Click* has three parts:

- The type of the form, *TForm1.*
- The name of the component, *RadioButton1.*
- The name of the event *Click.*

Some code must be added between the begin pair to change the colour of the text yellow when this event occurs. Only one line is needed:

> *Memo1.**Font.Color** := clYellow;*

The name of the memo component is *Memo1.* The **Font** property has several components, of which **Color** is one. To see all of the components of the Font property select the memo, select the **Font** property and double click on the '+' sign on the left of the property. **clYellow** is a constant which represents the colour yellow.

This process should be repeated for the other two buttons in this group. The constants which represent the olive and black colours are **clOlive** and **clBlack**. If you want to see what other colours you can assign to the text:

- Select the **Memo** component.
- Select the **Font** property.
- Double click on the '+' sign.
- Click on the down pointing arrow on the right of the **Color** property as shown in fig 4.5.

A list of possible colours is displayed. In addition to standard colours such as yellow and blue, you can use the colour which is currently assigned to a part of your Windows environment, such as the colour of an active caption, or a scroll bar. If you change these in your Windows environment they will automatically change in your application.

Fig 4.5 Changing the colour of text in a memo.

The full code for these three radio buttons which change the text colour is shown below:

```
procedure TForm1.RadioButton1Click(Sender: TObject);
begin
     Memo1.Font.Color := clYellow;
end;


procedure TForm1.RadioButton2Click(Sender: TObject);
begin
     Memo1.Font.Color := clOlive;
end;


procedure TForm1.RadioButton3Click(Sender: TObject);
begin
     Memo1.Font.Color := clBlack;
end;
```

When you have made these changes to your application try to run it. If you have made a typing error the Code window will be displayed with the problem line highlighted. There will be a message at the bottom of the window which gives you an idea of the error. The error messages are not always helpful and are sometimes misleading, so if an error does occur you should carefully check the syntax of the code you have typed. There may be more than one error to be corrected before the application runs. You should verify that this part of the application works correctly before making further changes. It is good practice when developing software to test small parts of your application and fix problems as soon as they occur.

Changing the background colour

The radio buttons which control the background colour are part of a **RadioGroup** component. The **Click** event handler for all of these buttons is the same, but you can determine which button has been pressed by testing the **ItemIndex** property. You should go to the template event handler which Delphi creates by selecting the component and double clicking on the **OnClick** event of the event page of the Object Inspector as before, but there is a quicker method. Simply double click on the component. The code needed in the event handler is shown below:

```
procedure TForm1.RadioGroup1Click(Sender: TObject);
begin
    If RadioGroup1.ItemIndex=0 then Memo1.Color := clRed;
    if RadioGroup1.ItemIndex=1 then Memo1.Color := clGreen;
    if RadioGroup1.ItemIndex=2 then Memo1.Color := clBlue;
    if RadioGroup1.ItemIndex=3 then Memo1.Color := clWhite;
end;
```

RadioGroup1 is the name of the component and **ItemIndex** is the name of the property we are testing. If it is zero, that is if the first radio button in the list is selected, the background colour is assigned to red. The **Color** property of the **Memo** component determines the background colour.

Changing the text size

A drop down combo box is used to control the size of the text. The size of the text is determined by a sub-property of the **Font** property of the memo, for example:

Memo1.Font.Size = 12;

assigns a font size of 12 points. The code that we need to write in the template procedure is a little more complicated, since we need to extract the size from the selected item in the combo box. The event which occurs when you select an item in a combo box is an **OnChange** event.

You can tell which item in a combo box has been selected by looking at the **ItemIndex** property. The first item in the list has an **ItemIndex** property of zero and so on. The text in the combo box which has been selected is available in the **Items** property, for example, if the third item in a combo box called *ComboBox1* is *'Paris'*, *ComboBox1*.**Items**[2] = *'Paris'*. Note the third item has an index of 2.

The item selected in the combo box in this application is therefore given by:

ComboBox1.Items[ComboBox1.ItemIndex]

The square brackets enclose the index number. This is a string value which must be converted to an integer, since the size of the font must be specified as an integer. The full event procedure is shown below:

```
procedure TForm1.ComboBox1Change(Sender: TObject);
begin
    Memo1.Font.Size :=
    StrToInt(ComboBox1.Items[ComboBox1.ItemIndex]);
end;
```

The assignment statement can be put onto one line, but it is less readable.

Changing the font

To change the font, you need to know what fonts are available for your screen. The number of fonts available is given by **Screen.Fonts.Count**. The name of the first font is given by **Screen.Fonts**[0], the name of the second font is given by **Screen.Fonts**[1], the name of the final font available is given by **Screen.Fonts[Screen.Fonts.Count - 1]**. The −1 is required since the first font has an index of zero.

To add an item to the **Items** property of the list box, which contains all the text in the list box use the **Add** method. The list box is best loaded when the form is created, that is when a **FormCreate** event occurs for the form. The event handler is shown below:

```
procedure TForm1.FormCreate(Sender: TObject);
var
    c : Integer;
begin
    for c := 0 to Screen.Fonts.Count - 1 do
        ListBox1.Items.Add(Screen.Fonts[c]);
end;
```

The first time this loop is executed, the variable *c* is zero. This adds the first font to *ListBox1*.**Items**. The second time, *c* is one and the second font is added and so on for all the available fonts.

If you want to know what fonts are available for your printer you should substitute the word **Printer** for **Screen** in this event procedure.

Italicising the text and closing the application

To italicise the text, the **Style** property of the memo must be changed. The event procedure for the click event for the check box is shown below.

```
procedure TForm1.CheckBox1Click(Sender: TObject);
begin
    if Memo1.Font.Style = [fsItalic] then Memo1.Font.Style:=[]
    else Memo1.Font.Style := [fsItalic]
end;
```

The style of text is tested to see if it is italic. If it is then it is made non-italic. If it is non-italic it is made italic.

The **OnClick** event handler for the button uses a **Close** statement to terminate the application. You can of course end the application in the usual way by clicking on the button with a cross on it, in the top right corner of the form. The code for this event is shown below:

```
procedure TForm1.Button1Click(Sender: TObject);
begin
    Close;
end;
```

The completed code

A minor refinement to the application is to set the **ItemIndex** property of the combo box to 1, so that this is displayed when the application is started and to assign the text size in the memo to this value. This is done in the **OnFormCreate** event handler. The completed code for this event for this application is shown below:

```
procedure TForm1.FormCreate(Sender: TObject);
var
    c : Integer;
begin
    Combobox1.ItemIndex := 1;
    Memo1.Font.Size :=
    StrToInt(ComboBox1.Items[ComboBox1.ItemIndex]);
    for c := 0 to Screen.Fonts.Count - 1 do
        ListBox1.Items.Add(Screen.Fonts[c]);
end;

procedure TForm1.RadioGroup1Click(Sender: TObject);
begin
    If RadioGroup1.ItemIndex=0 then Memo1.Color := clRed;
    if RadioGroup1.ItemIndex=1 then Memo1.Color := clGreen;
```

```
    if RadioGroup1.ItemIndex=2 then Memo1.Color := clBlue;
    if RadioGroup1.ItemIndex=3 then Memo1.Color := clWhite;
end;

procedure TForm1.Button1Click(Sender: TObject);
begin
    Close;
end;

procedure TForm1.ComboBox1Change(Sender: TObject);
begin
    Memo1.Font.Size :=
    StrToInt(ComboBox1.Items[ComboBox1.ItemIndex]);
end;

procedure TForm1.ListBox1Click(Sender: TObject);
begin
    Memo1.Font.Name := listBox1.Items[ListBox1.ItemIndex];
end;

procedure TForm1.CheckBox1Click(Sender: TObject);
begin
    if Memo1.Font.Style = [fsItalic] then Memo1.Font.Style:=[]
    else Memo1.Font.Style := [fsItalic]
end;

procedure TForm1.RadioButton1Click(Sender: TObject);
begin
    Memo1.Font.Color := clYellow;
end;

procedure TForm1.RadioButton2Click(Sender: TObject);
begin
    Memo1.Font.Color := clOlive;
end;

procedure TForm1.RadioButton3Click(Sender: TObject);
begin
    Memo1.Font.Color := clBlack;
end;
end.
```

An easier technique

The application we have developed works well, but it is not the standard way in which fonts and text styles are controlled in a Windows application. This is such a common activity that there is a special dialog box which you can use. If you have used any popular Windows applications you will have seen the dialog box, shown in fig 4.6, before.

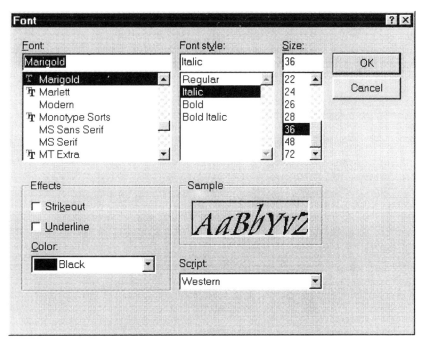

Fig 4.6 *The Font common dialog box.*

To use this dialog box, an application as shown in fig 4.7 is shown. The component above the button is a **FontDialog** which is on the Dialogs page of the Component Palette. It is not visible at run-time.

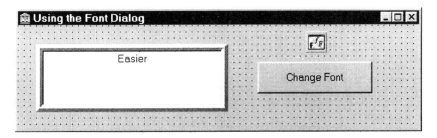

Fig 4.7 *The application at design time.*

To display the Font dialog, some Object Pascal must be added to the **Click** event of the button:

```
procedure TForm1.Button1Click(Sender: TObject);
begin
    FontDialog1.Font := Memo1.Font;
    FontDialog1.Execute;
    Memo1.Font := FontDialog1.Font;
end;
```

The current font attributes are assigned to the **Font** property of the dialog called *FontDialog1*. This is done so that when the Font dialog appears it will display the current attributes of the text in the memo. The **Execute** method displays the dialog. When you have chosen the properties that you want the memo to have, click on the OK button. The third line assigns the current properties of the dialog to the **Font** properties of the memo. The running application is shown in fig 4.8.

Fig 4.8 *The application at run-time.*

There are other dialogs which are used for controlling other standard features such as colour or printer characteristics, these are looked at in a later chapter.

5

The Additional Component Palette

Introduction

Delphi has a great range of components available in addition to thousands of components supplied by third parties. If possible use an existing component for your application. All of the commercially available components are thoroughly tested and it does make application writing faster, and less error prone. Applications using widely available components tend to have a more professional feel.

In this chapter we are going to look at:

- The components on the Additional page of the Component Palette.
- The key properties and events of these components.

We will be using these components throughout the later chapters of this book, so you can see how they are used in a variety of examples.

The BitBtn component

The bitmap button behaves in the same way as a command button, but you can display a bitmap on its face in addition to text.

   Fig 5.1 The BitBtn icon.

There is a range of standard images and text that you can use by specifying the **Kind** property and choosing one of the options. The buttons produced by all of these options are shown in fig 5.2.

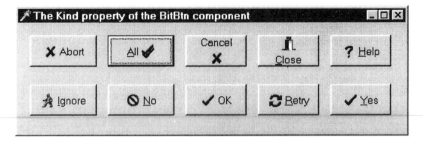

*Fig 5.2 The **Kind** property of the **BitBtn** button component.*

By default the bitmap is on the left of the text, but you can change this so that it is above, below or on the right of the text by using the **Layout** property.

You can display your own bitmap using the **Glyph** property. This overrides the **Kind** property, even if it is not set to **bkCustom**. Click on the button with three dots, which is on the right of the **Glyph** property and the Picture Editor as shown in fig 5.3 is displayed. Click on the **Load** button to browse for the bitmap you want.

Fig 5.3 The Picture Editor.

You can further control the position of the text by changing the distance between the bitmap and the text from its default of 4 pixels using the **Spacing** property. The **Margin** property controls the distance between the edge of the bitmap and the edge of the button.

The SpeedButton component

The **SpeedButton** component as shown in fig 5.4 has the same functionality as the command button except that it has an image alone on its face without any text.

Fig 5.4 The SpeedButton icon.

Speed buttons can also work together as a set. They are most commonly used to create a toolbar panel as shown in figure 5.5. To do this, add a panel to the form and then add as many speed buttons as required. These buttons will act as independent command buttons unless you assign the same non-zero value to the **GroupIndex** property of each of them. When this is done only one button of the group can be pressed at any one time. In fig 5.5 the centre button is pressed.

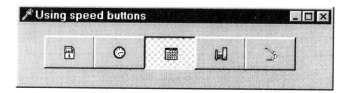

Fig 5.5 Using speed buttons on a panel.

Speed buttons do not have a caption property and so cannot display text, but they do have a **Glyph** property which allows you to add a bitmap image to the face of the button.

Speed buttons can be in three states:

- When the **Enabled** property is False, the button cannot be used, the button appears greyed as shown by the rightmost button in fig 5.5.
- When pressed the **Down** property is True, the middle button in fig 5.5.
- When not pressed the **Down** property is False, all the remaining buttons are in this state.

The MaskEdit component

The **MaskEdit** component, shown in fig 5.6 behaves like an **Edit** component and accepts a single line of input. Often you will know the format of input for a field, for example, if the application requests a telephone number only digits between 0 and 9 should be allowed. This component allows you to specify quite complicated formats for acceptable data.

Fig 5.6 The MaskEdit icon.

The property where you specify the edit mask is the **EditMask** property. Click on the button on the right of this property to see the Input Mask Editor window, shown in fig 5.7.

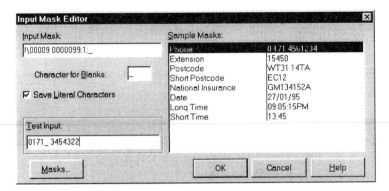

Fig 5.7 The Input Mask Editor.

There are different sample masks for different countries, the one shown here is for the UK.

Table 5.1 Special characters in the input mask.

Character	Meaning
!	Optional characters are represented as leading blanks, if this character is not present, optional characters are represented as trailing blanks.
>	All the following characters in the mask are uppercase.
<	All the following characters are lowercase.
<>	Upper and lowercase are both acceptable.
\	The character that follows it is literal, for example \3 means that the character 3 must be input at this point.
L	An alphabetic character is required, either uppercase or lowercase.
I	An alphabetic character is permitted, but it is not mandatory.
A	An alphabetic character is required.
a	An alphanumeric character is required, but is not mandatory.
C	An arbitrary character is required.
c	An arbitrary character is permitted but it is not mandatory.
0	A numeric character only is permitted.
9	A numeric character is permitted but it is not mandatory.
#	A numeric character or '+' or '–' is permitted but not required.
:	Separate hours, minutes and seconds. If you have specified a different character in your Windows set-up, that character is used instead.
/	Separates months, days and years, if you have specified a different character in your set-up, that is used instead.
_	Inserts spaces into the text, whenever one is placed in the mask a space is placed in the input text.
:	Separates the three fields of the mask.

The characters in the *Input Mask* have a specified meaning as shown in table 5.1.

These masks can be quite complicated to produce, so it is essential to thoroughly check that valid input is accepted and invalid is rejected.

The StringGrid component

This is a very useful component which allows you to display tabular information.

Fig 5.8 *The StringGrid icon.*

Each cell contains string data. This data cannot be specified at design time, you need to write some Object Pascal to load the data at run-time.

The **StringGrid** component can have some fixed rows and columns, which are shown in grey in fig 5.9. You can write to each cell (even the fixed ones) by using the **Cells** property and specifying the column and row. The cell in the top left has the co-ordinates of 0,0. Fig 5.9 shows the co-ordinates of each cell.

0,0	1,0	2,0	3,0	4,0
0,1	1,1	2,1	3,1	4,1
0,2	1,2	2,2	3,2	4,2
0,3	1,3	2,3	3,3	4,3

Using the StringGrid component

Fill grid

Fig 5.9 *Using the StringGrid component.*

The code for producing this application is shown below, note that the name of the **StringGrid** component has been changed from *StringGrid1* to *Grid1*:

```
procedure TForm1.Button1Click(Sender: TObject);
var
c, r : Integer;
begin

for c:= 0 to Grid1.ColCount do
    begin
    for r:= 0 to Grid1.RowCount do
```

```
        Grid1.Cells[c, r] := IntToStr(c) + ','+ IntToStr(r);
    end;
  end;
```

The number of columns is given by the **ColCount** property, similarly the number of rows is given by the **RowCount** property. Note in this example that the variables *c* and *r* are integers and must be converted to strings before being displayed using the **IntToStr** function. The number of fixed rows and columns is given by the **FixedRows** and the **FixedCols** property.

One obvious problem with the application shown in fig 5.9 is that the grid is surrounded by a white border. To remove this border, the overall size of the component given by the **Width** and **Height** properties must be assigned to the total size of the column and row widths. The code to do this is best executed when the form is created, that is in the **FormCreate** event:

```
        Grid1.Width := Grid1.ColCount * Grid1.DefaultColWidth;
        Grid1.Height := Grid1.RowCount * Grid1.DefaultRowHeight;
```

If you try this example and look closely, you will see that the overall size of the component is a little small, since the width of the lines between the cells has not been taken into account. You can do this by adding the following lines:

```
        Grid1.Width:=Grid1.Width+
            Grid1.GridLineWidth * Grid1.ColCount;
        Grid1.Height := Grid1.Height +
            Grid1.GridLineWidth * Grid1.RowCount;
```

The width of the lines between the cells is given by the **GridLineWidth** property. You can include scroll bars if you wish using the **ScrollBars** property

The DrawGrid component

The **DrawGrid** component shown in fig 5.10 is a subset of the **StringGrid** component. It lacks a few of the properties but requires fewer system resources.

                 Fig 5.10 The DrawGrid icon.

The **DrawGrid** component does not have the **Cells**, **Cols** and **Rows** properties and therefore is only useful in circumstances where you wish to simply display rather than manipulate data.

The Image component

The **Image** component is used to display images, all of the popular formats, including bitmap files (.BMP), icons (.ICO), Windows meta-files (.EMF) and extended Windows meta-files (EMF).

*Fig 5.11 The **Image** icon.*

The picture is specified in the **Picture** property. The Picture Editor allows you to browse for the picture you want. There are two particularly important properties that have a major impact on the way in which the pictures are displayed.

If the **Stretch** property is true, the image will fit exactly inside the frame of the component. This is shown in the right image of fig 5.12. If the **Stretch** property is not true, only a part of the image will be displayed as shown by the left image.

The **Stretch** property has no effect if the image specified is an icon.

*Fig 5.12 Using the **Stretch** property.*

If the **AutoSize** property is true the size of the image will change to accommodate the image exactly.

The Shape component

The Shape component is useful for displaying simple shapes. All of the shapes shown in fig 5.14 are **Shape** components. It is the **Shape** property which determines which is displayed.

*Fig 5.13 The **Shape** icon.*

The colour and style of the shape border is determined by the **Pen** properties.

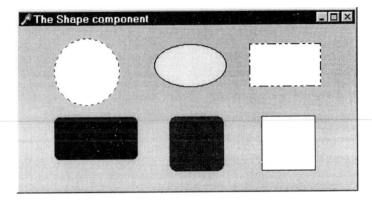

*Fig 5.14 The **Shape** property of the **Image** component.*

The colour of the interior of the shape is controlled by the **Brush** property. This property allows you to choose a range of different fill patterns as shown in fig 5.15.

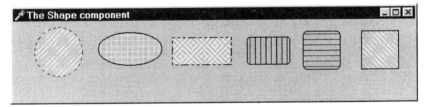

*Fig 5.15 The **Brush** property of the **Image** component.*

The Bevel component

The **Bevel** component is one of the simplest and least interesting of the Delphi components since it is used simply to improve the appearance of your application.

                    *Fig 5.16 The **Bevel** icon.*

A bevel can appear as one of the following, depending on the value of its **Shape** property:

Table 5.2 *The value of the **Shape** property.*

Value	Meaning
bsBox	The area within the **Bevel** is raised or lowered, depending on whether the **Style** property is **bsRaised** or **bsLowered**.
bsFrame	The area has a raised or lowered outline.
bsTopLine	A single line at the top of the bevel.
bsBottomLine	A single line at the bottom.
bsLeftLine	A single line on the left.
bsRightLine	A single line on the right.

Fig 5.17 shows a few **Bevel** components.

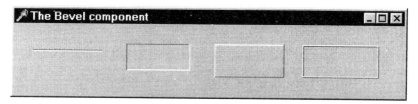

Fig 5.17 *The **Bevel** component.*

The ScrollBox component

Scroll boxes are used as containers for other components in the same way as **Panel** components. The key difference is that you can view an area larger than the area of the component by scrolling horizontally and vertically.

   Fig 5.18 *The **ScrollBox** icon.*

Fig 5.19 shows an **Image** component within a scroll box which is too large to be completely viewed at any one time, but which can be viewed in sections using the scroll bars.

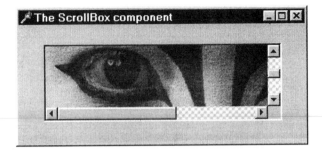

*Fig 5.19 Using the **ScrollBox** component.*

The CheckListBox component

The **CheckListBox** component behaves in the same way as a **ListBox** component, but each entry in the list has a checkbox adjacent to it.

                    *Fig 5.20 The **CheckListBox** icon.*

The items in the list are determined by the **Items** property. You enter the text which is adjacent to the checkbox using the String list editor.

The **Checked** and **State** properties indicate if a list item is checked or not. If **Checked** is True, the **State** is **dbChecked**. If **Checked** is False, the **State** could either be **cbUnchecked** or **cbGrayed**.

The Splitter component

This component creates a set of panes on a form which can be resized at run-time.

                    *Fig 5.21 The **Splitter** icon.*

In fig 5.22 all of the **Splitter** components have the **Align** property set to **AlLeft** except for the rightmost component which has an **Align** value of **AlClient**. This ensures that it will automatically expand to the right hand side of the form.

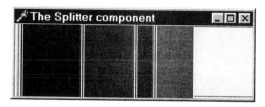

*Fig 5.22 Using the **Splitter** component.*

The **Color** property of each of the five **Splitter** components has been changed for greater clarity.

The StaticText component

This component behaves in a similar way to a **Label** component, except that it has some extra features such as a variety of border styles.

  *Fig 5.23 The **StaticText** icon.*

The Chart component

The **Chart** component is only one aspect of TeeChart Pro version 3, which can be bought separately and gives even more flexibility. **DBChart** is a data aware version of this component which can use a database as its data source.

  *Fig 5.24 The **Chart** icon.*

This is an extremely powerful tool, which is supported by a lot of on-line help. **Chart** is able to take raw data and present it in a graphical form.

To create a chart:

* Add the **Chart** component to a form.
* Right click on the component to display its speed-menu.
* Select the **Edit Chart** option. The tabbed dialog shown in fig 5.25 is displayed.

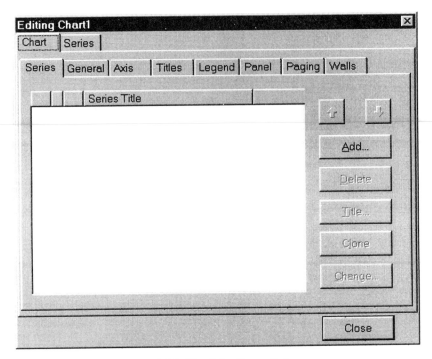

Fig 5.25 The Edit Chart dialog.

Click on the **Add** button to display the dialog shown in fig 5.26.

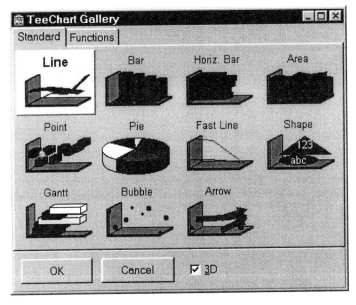

Fig 5.26 Selecting the chart type.

- Select the type of chart that you want by clicking on it. In this example choose the Pie chart.
- Click on the **OK** button to return to the Edit Chart dialog.
- Select the Titles page to change the title (not the **Title** button). In this example I have *Working Activities of People between 18 and 60*.
- Click on the **Close** button.
- Click on the **Close** button in the Edit Chart dialog.
- Add three **Edit** components, four **Label** components and a **Button** component to your application which looks like the one shown in fig 5.27.

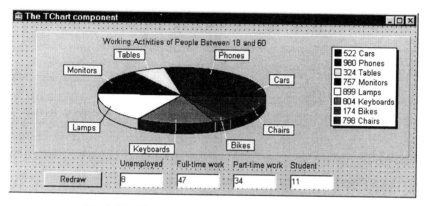

Fig 5.27 The charting application at design time.

The chart displayed is inserted by TeeChart to illustrate what your application will look like at run-time.

To display your own data, which is input using the four **Edit** components we need to write some code in the **OnClick** event handler for the button:

```
procedure TForm2.RedrawClick(Sender: TObject);
begin
      Series1.AddPie(StrToInt(Edit1.Text), 'age 18-25', clGreen);
      Series1.AddPie(StrToInt(Edit2.Text), 'age 25-35', clRed);
      Series1.AddPie(StrToInt(Edit3.Text), 'age 35-45', clWhite);
      Series1.AddPie(StrToInt(Edit4.Text), 'age over 45', clBlue);
end;
```

This code will update the chart when it is executed and will produce the chart shown in fig 5.28.

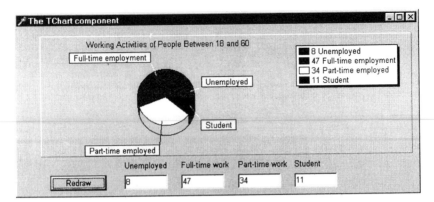

***Fig 5.28** The charting application at run-time.*

There is also a wizard to help you draw charts, select the **New | File** menu option and select the Business page. You will see an icon for the TeeChart Wizard.

6
Displaying and Reading Text

Introduction

One of the most common ways of displaying text and receiving input is to use a dialog box. Dialog boxes are useful pop-up windows which are often informative with only an OK button, but they can be more complicated with a range of buttons and they may even request you to type some text. Often a date, a time, or a number needs to be shown. If you do not specify the format you want, Delphi will use a sensible default. However you do have complete control over how it is displayed.

In this chapter you will learn about:

- Displaying dialog boxes.
- Creating customised dialog boxes.
- Formatting dates and times.
- Formatting numbers.

The ShowMessage procedure

The simplest way of displaying a message is to use the **ShowMessage** procedure. A modal message box is displayed in response to the procedure call, for example, as shown in fig 6.1.

> *ShowMessage ('Press the OK button to Continue');*

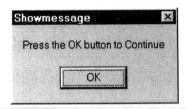

Fig 6.1 The ShowMessage procedure.

The name of your application's executable file is used as the title. The dialog box automatically appears in the centre of the screen, if you want to control its position explicitly, use the **ShowMessagePos** procedure. This is the same as the **ShowMessage** procedure except that the X and Y co-ordinates of the top left of the dialog box are specified, for example:

> *ShowMessagePos('Ok to Continue?', 200, 500);*

The MessageDlg function

If you want to display a message and also collect input, you need to use the **MessageDlg** function. This function is more complicated than the **ShowMessage** procedure; however, it allows greater flexibility. There are four parameters, but they are not all mandatory:

- The text in the message box.
- The caption on the title bar and the graphic.
- The type of buttons displayed.
- A link to a Help topic.

There are four types of captions and graphics shown in table 6.1.

Table 6.1 Message box captions and graphics.

Value	Graphic	Value	Graphic
mtWarning	⚠	mtError	❌
mtInformation	ⓘ	mtConfirmation	❓

The caption for **mtWarning** is *Warning* and so on. If you choose a fifth type, **mtCaption,** no bitmap is displayed and the message box caption is the name of the executable file.

There are nine different buttons that you can display by specifying **mbYes**, **mbNo**, **mbOK**, **mbCancel**, **mbHelp**, **mbAbort**, **mbRetry**, **mbIgnore**, **mbAll**. You can specify as many buttons as you wish, for example:

MessageDlg('Error', mtError, [mbRetry, mbCancel], 0);

The dialog produced is shown in fig 6.2.

Contrary to the Delphi Help, these buttons do not contain graphics of the type shown in the previous chapter in fig 5.2.

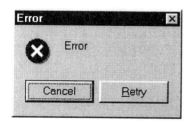

*Fig 6.2 The **MessageDlg** function.*

Note the square brackets around the parameter specifying the buttons, since this parameter is a set. There are some pre-defined sets for commonly used groups of buttons: **mbOkCancel**, **mbAbortRetryIgnore** and **mbYesNoCancel**. You do not need to enclose these in square brackets, for example:

MessageDlg('Disk error', mtWarning, mbAbortRetryIgnore, 0);

This produces the dialog shown in fig 6.3.

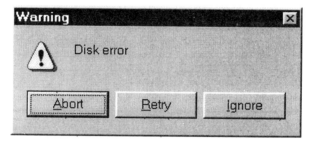

Fig 6.3 Using pre-defined button groups.

The **MessageDlg** function positions the dialog box in the centre in the same way as the **ShowMessage** procedure. If you want to control its position you must use the **MessageDlgPos** function. This is the same as the **MessageDlg** function except that the X and Y co-ordinates of the top left of the dialog box are an additional two parameters.

What button was pressed?

You usually need to know what button has been pressed, so that you can take appropriate action. The **MessageDlg** function returns a value which indicates this. The possible return values are : **mrNone, mrOk, mrCancel, mrAbort, mrRetry, mrIgnore, mrYes, mrNo, mrAll**. The code shown below writes a message to an **Edit** component, which indicates which button has been pressed.

> *begin*
>   *If MessageDlg('Error',**mtError**,[**mbOK**,**mbCancel**],0)=**mrOk** then*
>   *Edit1.text := 'OK button' else Edit1.text := 'Cancel button';*

Creating input forms

There are two dialog boxes which can be used to prompt for input, using two functions, **InputBox** and **InputQuery**.

The **InputBox** function has three parameters:

*Table 6.2 Parameters of the **InputBox** function.*

Parameter	Meaning
ACaption	The caption of the dialog box.
APrompt	The text adjacent to the edit box where the user types the input text.
ADefault	The text that is displayed in the edit box when the dialog box is first displayed.

The value returned is a string. These dialog boxes always have an **OK** and a **Cancel** button. The code below produces the dialog shown in fig 6.4.

> *var*
>   *F: String;*
> *begin*
>   *F:= InputBox('Folder?', 'Specify Folder','C:\DevStudio\Bin');*
> *end;*

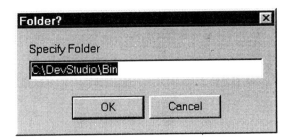

*Fig 6.4 The **InputBox** function.*

If the **OK** button is pressed the text in the edit box is returned, if the **Cancel** button is used, the default text is returned. You cannot tell which button has been pressed. If you do need to know this, you must use the **InputQuery** function. The return value is a boolean value. If this is true, the **OK** button was pressed, if False the **Cancel** button was chosen.

Standard dialog boxes

Delphi has a range of standard dialog boxes that you can create by selecting the **File** | **New** menu option and choose the **Dialogs** page as shown in fig 6.5.

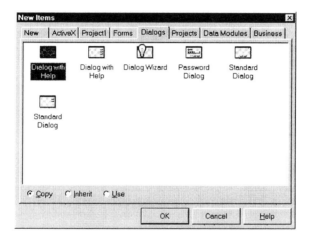

Fig 6.5 *Creating a standard dialog.*

There are two Help dialogs, one of which is shown in fig 6.6.

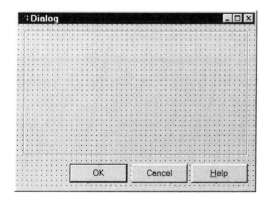

Fig 6.6 *The Help dialog.*

The only difference between the two Help dialogs is the position of the buttons. This dialog consists of a small number of standard components, in this case, three buttons and a bevel.

The most useful of the standard dialog boxes is the Password dialog, shown in fig 6.7. The **PasswordChar** property of the edit box is set to '*', so that whatever is typed appears as asterisks.

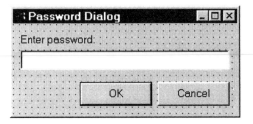

Fig 6.7 The Password dialog.

The standard dialog boxes are the same as the two help dialogs, but without the Help button.

The Dialog Wizard is useful in creating simple dialogs using a question and answer format, perhaps the most useful aspect is that you can create dialogs with a **PageControl** component and as many **TabSheet** components as required. To do this choose the *Multi-page, using Page control* option when prompted by the wizard. The example shown in fig 6.8 has three pages. The text is typed into a **Memo** component on each of the pages, which appears when its page tab is selected. The colour of the memo is the same as the **TabSheet** component it sits on and they have no border.

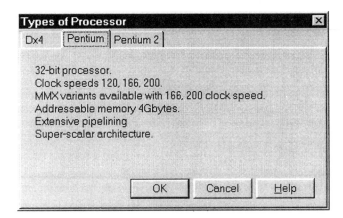

Fig 6.8 A multi-page dialog.

To display a dialog from an existing form you need to use the **Show** method, for example to show a dialog called *Form2* from *Form1*, the line:

Form1.Show;

is required. This is dealt with in detail in the next chapter.

Displaying dates and times

We have seen how to display text and numbers using **Edit** and **Memo** components, either as part of a dialog or simply on a form within an application. When you want to display information in an edit box or a memo, you need to convert it to a string. Delphi provides a powerful set of functions which allow you to do this:

- **DateTimeToStr** converts a date and time from the internal type **TDateTime** into a string.
- **StrToDateTime** converts a string into **TDateTime** format.

A useful function is **Now** which returns the current date and time.

When displaying a date and time, you can rely on Delphi to apply a default formatting standard on how the date is shown, however you can control every aspect of how the date and time is displayed using the **FormatDateTime** function. A few examples are shown in fig 6.9.

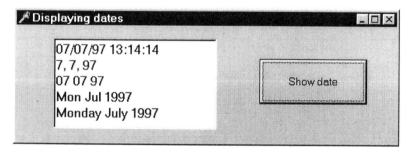

Fig 6.9 Displaying dates.

The code used to produce this is shown below:

```
procedure TForm1.Button1Click(Sender: TObject);
begin
  Memo1.Lines[0] := DateTimeToStr(Now);
  Memo1.Lines[1] := FormatDateTime('d, m, yy', Now);
  Memo1.Lines[2] := FormatDateTime('dd mm yy', Now);
  Memo1.Lines[3] := FormatDateTime('ddd mmm yyyy', Now);
  Memo1.Lines[4] := FormatDateTime('dddd mmmm yyyy', Now);
end;
```

The meaning of the d, m and y specifiers is shown in table 6.3:

Table 6.3 The d, m and y specifiers.

Specifier	Meaning
d	The day is displayed as a single number without a leading zero.
dd	The day has a leading zero.
ddd	Uses an abbreviated form for the day (Sun-Sat).
dddd	Uses a long day format (Sunday-Saturday).
ddddd	Displays the date in the form specified by the **ShortFormat** variable.
dddddd	Displays the date in the form specified by the **LongFormat** variable.
m	Displays the month without a leading zero.
mm	The month has a leading zero.
mmm	The abbreviated form of the month is used (Jan-Dec).
mmmm	The full month form is used (January-December).
yy	Two digit year (00-99).
yyyy	Four digit year (0000-9999).

Similar specifiers are used for displaying the time as shown in table 6.4:

Table 6.4 The h, s and t specifiers.

Specifier	Meaning
h	The hour is displayed without a leading zero.
hh	The hour has a leading zero.
n	The minute without a leading zero.
nn	The minute with a leading zero.
s	The second without a leading zero.
ss	The second with a leading zero.

In addition you can use the a/p specifiers to display a 12-hour clock time with an 'a' after all 'am' times and a 'p' after all 'pm' times. The 'a' or 'p' may be either upper or lowercase depending the case of the specifier. Similarly the am/pm specifier may be used to display 'am' or 'pm'.

When you are specifying a date to the **StrToDateTime** function you should separate the days, months and years with '/' characters and the hours, minutes and seconds with ':' characters, for example '15/7/97 11:25' is a valid date. You can use the specifiers, for example the code:

```
Memo1.Lines[0] := FormatDateTime('"Delphi 6 available "
dddd d mmmm yy ' + '"at" hh:nn am/pm',
StrToDateTime('2/3/99 10:30'));
```

produces the date as shown in fig 6.10.

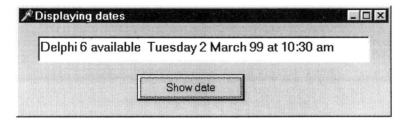

Fig 6.10 Rumours of Delphi version 6 release!

Note that if you are in Europe, 2/3 is the 2nd March, while in the US it is the 3rd February. This is controlled by the Control Panel setting for your computer.

If you are working with a date without a time, you can use the **DatetoStr** function, similarly if you are using a time without a date you can use the **TimeToStr** function to convert to a string. There are also functions for converting the other way predictably called **StrToDate** and **StrToTime**.

Displaying numbers

We have already seen the **StrToInt** and **IntToStr** functions for converting between strings and integers, if you are working with floating point numbers you can use the corresponding functions **StrToFloat** and **FloatToStr**. You can control how a numeric field is displayed using the **Format** function. A few examples are shown in the code below.

```
Memo1.Lines[0] := FloatToStr(1234.5678);
Memo1.Lines[1] := Format('%12.3f',[1234.5678]);
Memo1.Lines[2] := Format('%12.6f',[1234.5678]);
Memo1.Lines[3] := Format('%6.3e',[1234.5678]);
Memo1.Lines[4] := Format('%5.3n',[1234.5678]);
```

This code produces the numbers shown in fig 6.11.

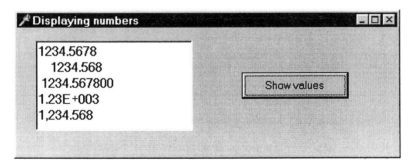

*Fig 6.11 Displaying numbers using **Format**.*

The most important format specifiers have the following meaning:

Table 6.5 *The h, s and t specifiers.*

Specifier	Meaning
d	Decimal. The value must be an integer. The Delphi help indicates that if the number of characters is less than the number required, the string has leading zeros, in fact leading zeros are not inserted.
e	Scientific. The value is presented in the form "d.dd..E+ddd". There is always one digit before the decimal point and three after the 'E'. A default of 2 digits after the decimal point is assumed if not specified.
f	Fixed. The value must be a floating point format. The number is presented in the form "dddd.dd ". If not specified two digits after the decimal point are assumed.
g	General. The value must be a floating point format. The shortest possible representation is used, either fixed or scientific. A default of 15 digits is assumed if not specified. A decimal point is used only if necessary.
n	Number. The same format as the "f" specifier, except that the thousands are separated by commas.
m	Money. The value must be a floating point format. The format is controlled by the International section of the Windows Control Panel.
x	Hexadecimal. The value must be an integer. It is expressed in hexadecimal.

A useful feature of **Format** is that you can change the precision at run-time. The following two lines produce the same output:

> ***Format('%5.2', [1234.5678]);***
> ***Format('*.*f', [8, 2, 1234.5678]);***

The *.* in the specifier indicates that the first two values in the list (in this case 8 and 2) are to be substituted into the specifier. You could replace these two constants by variables and set their values at run-time.

7
Using Forms

Introduction

All of the applications that we have looked at so far have used only one form, but most real applications use many forms. Delphi has an excellent set of tools for creating and using forms, as well as many useful standard forms. Many applications use an MDI (Multiple Document Interface), where a form creates child forms which exist within it. Delphi itself makes extensive use of MDI forms.

In this chapter you will learn how to:

- Create forms.
- Use modal and modeless forms.
- Use standard forms.
- Create and use MDI forms.

Creating new forms

When you start a new application, Delphi automatically adds a single form. If you want to add another form to your application select the **File | New Form** menu option. The forms that you add in this way have default property values and no components.

Delphi also has a set of useful form templates which you can add to your application by choosing the **File | New** option and displaying the **Forms** page as shown in fig 7.1.

There are three ways to include these forms in your project, based on the three radio buttons at the base of the form in fig 7.1:

- **Copy**. An exact copy of the item is included in the project. If either the template or the copy are changed, the other is not affected. The two forms are completely independent.
- **Inherit**. A new class is created which is added to your project. If the template is changed, any changes will be reflected in your inherited form

when you recompile. Any changes that you make to your inherited form will not affect the template form.

- **Use**. The form is used directly as if it had been created as a part of that project. If you change the form all other projects which use this form will change when they are compiled.

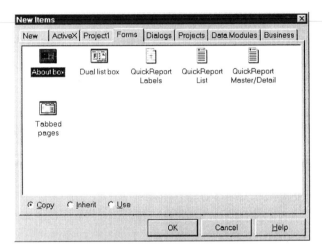

Fig 7.1 Adding a standard form to an application.

For forms the most widely used option is **Copy**.

One of the most useful forms is the Dual List Box, which is shown in fig 7.2. The unit file for this form also includes the code to make the form fully functioning. When you click on a button with a single arrow, the selected items are moved to the other list box. Clicking on a button with two arrows moves all the entries.

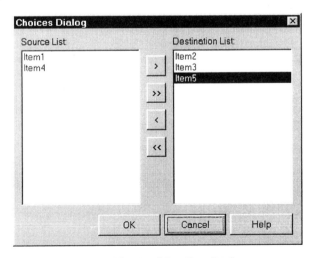

Fig 7.2 The Dual List Box Dialog.

If you want to try this for yourself, you must first add the form to your project. If you then run the application the usual *Form1* will appear. If you want the dual list box form to appear directly select the **Project | Options** menu option. Display the **Forms** page and make *DualListDlg* the main form. The main form is the one which appears when the application is run.

Another popular form is the About Box which every professional application must include. This is shown in fig 7.3.

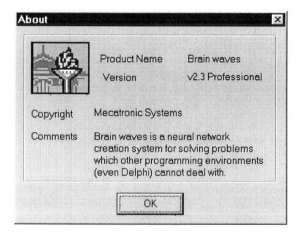

Fig 7.3 *The About Box.*

In this figure the text describing the product has been added by using a memo for the **Comments** and edit boxes for the other entries. The **BorderStyle** property of each was assigned to **bsNone** and the **Color** property to the same as the background of the **Panel** component.

Finding forms

When you have more than one form in your application it is easy to lose forms and be unable to find them. The best way to find the form you want is to use the **View | Forms** menu option and to choose the form that you want to see. A quick way of doing this is to press **Shift+F12**. If you have the unit code for the form you want displayed, you can select the **View | Toggle Form/Unit** option or press **F12**. Most Delphi programmers do remember these two shortcut keys, since they are so commonly used. The other shortcut key that most people use is **F11**, which displays the Object Inspector.

Modal and modeless forms

Forms can be either modal or modeless:

- A modal form must be closed before the focus can be switched to another window. You can do this by clicking on the top left corner of the box or by clicking on one of the dialog box buttons and causing it to close itself. Most dialog boxes are modal.
- A modeless form allows the user to switch to another window.

At design time dialog boxes are neither modal or modeless; this property is controlled at run-time.

Displaying forms

When you run an application, the form specified as your main form on the Forms page of the **Project | Options** menu is displayed. In order to display other forms you need to use one of two methods:

- **Show**. This method displays a modeless form.
- **ShowModal**. This method displays a modal form.

Most dialogs are modal while most forms are modeless.

If you want to make a form invisible use the **Hide** method. The application shown in fig 7.4 has two forms. Clicking on the button on *Form1* makes *Form2* appear and *Form1* disappear. Similarly *Form2* can be hidden and *Form1* displayed by clicking on the button on *Form2*.

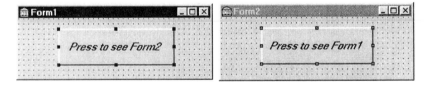

Fig 7.4 *Showing and hiding forms.*

The only code needed in the **OnClick** event for the two buttons is:

> *Form1.**Hide**;*
> *Form1.**Show**;*

for the *Form1* button and:

> *Form2.**Hide**;*
> *Form1.**Show**;*

for the *Form2* button.

When you try and run this application the first time, a warning message as shown in fig 7.5 will be shown.

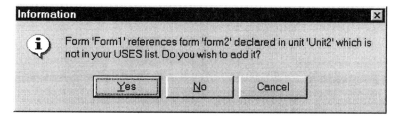

Fig 7.5 Warning message.

If you click on *Yes*, Delphi will correct the problem for you. If you try to run it a second time, it will produce a similar message about the reference to *Form1* from *Unit2*, the unit file for *Form2*. You can click on *Yes* and Delphi will also correct this problem. When you try for the third time to run this application, it will compile correctly and behave as expected. While it is good to know that Delphi has corrected a problem it spotted in your application it is important to know what is going on. To do this we need to look in more detail at the structure of a unit file.

Unit files

All forms have a unit file with an extension of PAS associated with them. The unit file contains all of the event procedures for the form and any other procedures that are used by the event procedures. If, for example, several of the event procedures need to sort numbers in order of size, it is more efficient to write one sorting procedure and to call it from each event procedure that needs it. This avoids duplication code and helps to keep errors to a minimum.

All units have the same basic structure:

> **unit** *<identifier>;*
> **interface**
> **uses** *<list of units>*
>   *{optional}*
>   *{ Public declarations }*
> **implementation**
> **uses** *<list of units>*
>   *{optional}*
>   *{ Private declarations }*
>   *{ procedures & functions implementation}*
> **initialization**   *{optional}*
> **end***;*

The reserved word unit is followed by an identifier which gives the name of the unit, for example, *Unit1*.

The keyword **interface** marks the start of the interface section which declares parts of the unit which are visible to other units. Any code in the current unit can access the declarations in the interface part of another unit by specifying those units in the following **uses** clause. The **uses** clause lists PAS files (including unit files).

What this means is that if your code in *Unit1* wants to refer to a procedure or form in another unit, you need to list that unit name in the **uses** clause. If you want a procedure in one unit to be used by a procedure in another unit you need to list that procedure in the interface section of the unit where the procedure exists.

The best way to understand this is to see how it is used in practice. In this example there are two forms shown in fig 7.6.

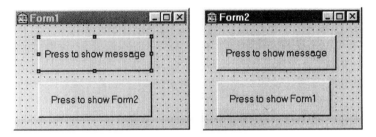

Fig 7.6 *The application at design time.*

Each form has a button which hides itself and displays the other form as in the previous example. The unit file *Unit1* also has a procedure called *MyMessage* which displays a message box. This procedure is also called from *Unit2*. The complete listing for *Unit1* is shown below:

```
unit Unit1;
interface
uses
Windows, Messages, SysUtils, Classes, Graphics, Controls, Forms, Dialogs,
StdCtrls;
procedure MyMessage;
type
     TForm1 = class(TForm)
          Button1: TButton;
          Button2: TButton;
          procedure Button1Click(Sender: TObject);
          procedure Button2Click(Sender: TObject);
     private
     public
     end;

     var
     Form1: TForm1;
implementation
     uses Unit2
procedure MyMessage;
```

```
begin
    ShowMessage('This is MyMessage');
end;

procedure TForm1.Button1Click(Sender: TObject);
begin
    MyMessage;
end;

procedure TForm1.Button2Click(Sender: TObject);
begin
    Form1.Hide;
    Form2.Show;
end;
end.
```

This is the listing for *Unit2*.

```
unit Unit2;
interface
uses
Windows, Messages, SysUtils, Classes, Graphics, Controls, Forms, Dialogs,
StdCtrls;
type
    TForm2 = class(TForm)
        Button1: TButton;
        Button2: TButton;
        procedure Button1Click(Sender: TObject);
        procedure Button2Click(Sender: TObject);
    private
    { Private declarations }
    public
    { Public declarations }
    end;

var
    Form2: TForm2;
implementation
    uses Unit1;
procedure TForm2.Button1Click(Sender: TObject);
begin
    MyMessage;
end;

procedure TForm2.Button2Click(Sender: TObject);
begin
```

> *Form2.Hide;*
> *Form1.Show;*
> *end;*
> *end.*

If you have not looked in detail at a unit file before, the usual reaction is to panic, in fact you only need to add a few lines to the code generated by Delphi to get the application working.

In *Unit1*, the **OnClick** event for *Button2* calls the **Hide** and **Show** method as before. The **OnClick** event for *Button1* calls the procedure **MyMessage**. This procedure is defined immediately above the event procedures. Note that it must be placed before any calls to it.

Similarly in *Unit2*, the **OnClick** events are virtually identical.

The code is now complete, but *Unit2* does not know which unit the procedure *MyMessage* is in or where *Form1* is defined. *Unit1* does not know where *Form2* is defined and must inform other units that it contains the *MyMessage* procedure.

Form1 lists *Unit2* in its **uses** clause. *Form2* lists *Unit1* in its **uses** clause. This takes care of the references to the forms. *Form1* lists *MyMessage* in its interface section. This solves all the problems of unresolved references and completes the application.

The Dialogs page

The Dialogs page of the Component Palette, shown in fig 7.7, contains some extremely useful common dialogs, which are widely used in virtually every Windows application.

Fig 7.7 The Dialogs page of the Component Palette.

These components are placed on a form in the usual way, but are not visible at run-time, so their position does not matter. To display the dialog use the **Execute** method, for example:

> *ReplaceDialog1.Execute;*

displays the replace dialog. We are going to look at each of these in turn.

The OpenDialog component

The **OpenDialog** component is the standard way of browsing through your file system and opening files.

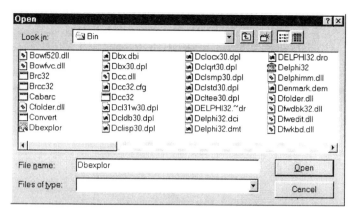

*Fig 7.8 The **OpenDialog** component.*

You can control the types of fields which are displayed by using the **Filter** property. Clicking on the three dots adjacent to this property in the Object Inspector displays the Filter Editor shown in fig 7.9.

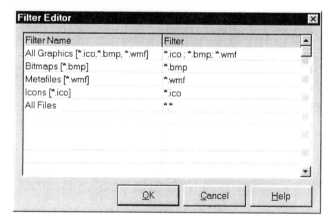

Fig 7.9 The Filter Editor.

The text in the left column is text that you see when you run the application as a label to the *Files of Type* edit box, shown in fig 7.8. The right column lists the types of files which are displayed. If more than one type is required, separate the items by semicolons.

The **FileName** property of the dialog is the name of the last selected file. The **Files** property is a list of strings which lists all of the files in the folder which match the wild card specification. The first entry, that is **Files**[0] contains the same string as the **FileName** property.

The SaveDialog component

The **SaveDialog** component has virtually the same set of properties as the **OpenDialog** component.

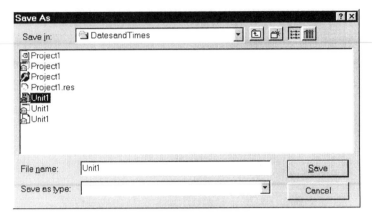

*Fig 7.10 The **SaveDialog** component.*

When the **Save** button is clicked the **FileName** property contains the name of the file selected.

The OpenPictureDialog component

This component is virtually the same as the **OpenDialog** component, except that it displays a pre-view picture of the currently selected image file.

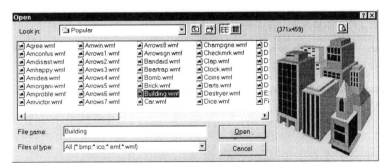

*Fig 7.11 The **OpenPictureDialog** component.*

The graphics file types which are supported include bitmap (*.BMP), Windows metafiles (*.WMF), enhanced Windows metafiles (*.EMF) and Icons (*.ICO). If the current file is not a supported format, 'None' is displayed in the pre-view region.

The SavePictureDialog component

The **SavePictureDialog** component behaves in a very similar manner to the **SaveDialog** component, except that there is a region which displays the currently selected image file.

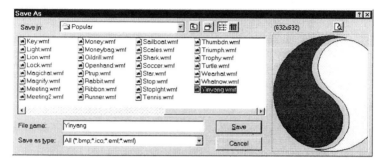

*Fig 7.12 The **SavePictureDialog** component.*

The same range of graphics files are supported.

The FontDialog component

The majority of Windows applications, including Delphi, use the **FontDialog** component, so this dialog should be familiar.

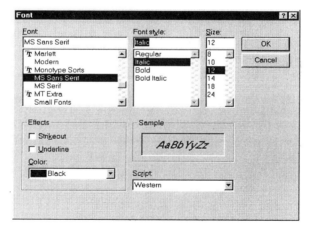

*Fig 7.13 The **FontDialog** component.*

The selected font is specified in the **Font** property. This property is made up of many sub-properties, for example the name. You can address the name of the font selected for a *FontDialog1* as *FontDialog1*.**Font**.**Name**.

The ColorDialog component

The **ColorDialog** component is also used in numerous places in Delphi, wherever you want to change a colour visually, rather than just selecting it from a descriptive list.

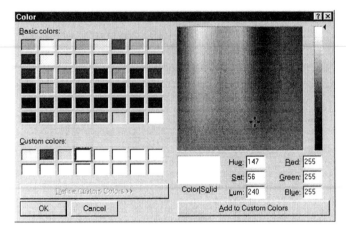

*Fig 7.14 The **ColorDialog** component.*

The selected colour is stored in the **Color** property. Colours are stored in terms of their red, green and blue components. Each of these components is stored in 8 bits and is therefore an integer between 0 and 255.

When this dialog first appears, only the left side of the dialog shown in fig 7.12 is visible. Click on the *Define Custom Color* button to display the right side of the dialog.

The **Options** property controls many aspects of the dialog box. There are five parts to this property.

*Table 7.1 The **Options** properties of the **ColorDialog** component.*

Value	Meaning
cdFullOpen	Shows the custom colours when the dialog first opens.
cdPreventFullOpen	Disables the *Define Custom Color* button.
cdHelpShow	A Help button is added.
cdSolidColor	Windows uses the nearest solid colour to the one chosen.
cdAnyColor	Non-solid colours may be selected.

The default value for all of these properties is False.

The PrintDialog component

This is the standard Windows dialog for printing and includes a wide range of properties which support all of the powerful features we have grown used to in Windows applications.

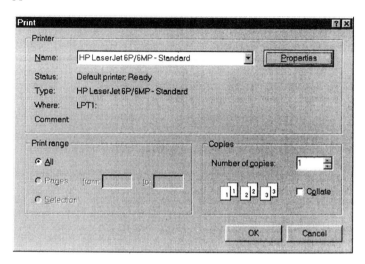

*Fig 7.15 The **PrintDialog** component.*

The most commonly used of the properties of this dialog are shown in table 7.2.

***Table 7.2** Common properties of the **PrintDialog** component.*

Property	Meaning
Collate	A Boolean which is True if multiple copies are to be collated.
Copies	The number of copies to be printed. If it is zero, one copy is printed.
FromPage	The starting page of the print job.
MaxPage	The greatest page number that can be printed.
MinPage	The smallest page number which can be printed.
PrintRange	If the value is **prAllPages**, the *All* radio button is selected. If **prSelection**, the *Selection* radio button is selected. If **prPageNums**, the *Pages* radio button is selected.
PrintToFile	A Boolean, if True it indicates that the *Print to File* check box is selected.
ToPage	The finishing page of the print job.

This dialog box, in common with the others, collects information about what you want to happen, for example completing this dialog box and clicking on the *OK* button does not actually print the job, but it provides full information on what sort of print job you want to carry out. Some additional code must be written to send the information to the printer.

The PrinterSetupDialog component

This dialog box allows you to change every aspect of your printer. It is shown in fig 7.16.

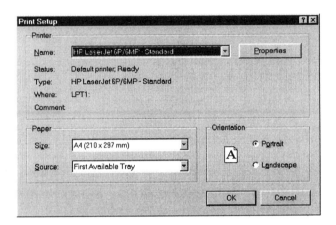

*Fig 7.16 The **PrinterSetupDialog** component.*

The FindDialog component

This is a standard dialog box for searching through text, it is used in many applications including Delphi. The position of this dialog is given by the **Position** property. For compatibility with older applications the **Left** and **Top** property are maintained although the values of these properties are embodied in the **Position** property. The **Left** and **Top** properties should not be used as there is no guarantee that they will be included in later versions of Delphi.

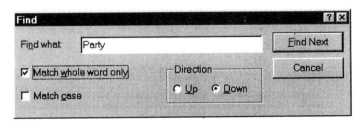

*Fig 7.17 The **FindDialog** component.*

The text which you are searching for is stored in the **FindText** property. The **Options** property contains thirteen parts which control aspects of the search. They are listed in the Delphi Help if you look on the Index page for **TFindDialog** and choose **Options** in the sub-list.

The ReplaceDialog component

The dialog has virtually identical properties to the **FindDialog** dialog. In addition it has the **ReplaceText** property which contains the text which will replace the text in the **FindText** property.

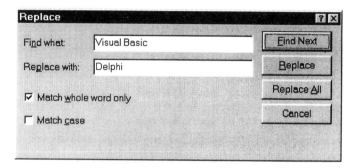

Fig 7.18 The ReplaceDialog component.

SDI and MDI forms

All of the forms that we have looked at so far have been SDI (Single Document Interface) forms. In many applications you can also have MDI (Multiple Document Interface) forms. An MDI form can have child forms which are displayed within the parent form.

Table 7.3 The FormStyle property of forms.

Value	Meaning
fsNormal	The form is SDI.
fsMDIForm	The form is an MDI parent form.
fsMDIChild	The form is an MDI child form.
fsStayOnTop	The form is SDI and stays on top of all other open forms.

Forms have a property called **FormStyle**, which is used to determine if a form is SDI or MDI. The **FormStyle** property has four possible values as shown in table 7.3.

Creating parent and child forms

In order to create a parent form and four child forms:

- Start a new project.
- Use the **New Form** option from the **File** menu to create four new blank forms.
- Select the **View Forms** from the **View** menu and select *Form1*. This displays the form first created. This is going to be the MDI parent form.
- Click on the Properties page of the Object Inspector and set the **FormStyle** property to **fsMDIForm.**
- Select the other three forms in turn and set their **FormStyle** properties to **fsMDIChild.**

If no Pascal code is written and the application is run, all four of the child forms are shown cascaded on the parent form.

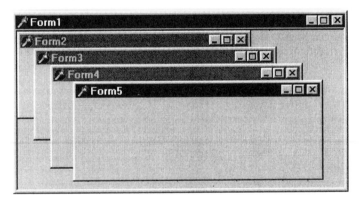

Fig 7.19 Parent and child forms.

Only one file in an application can have a **FormStyle** property of **fsMDIForm**, and this must be the main form. This means that you can only have one MDI form in an application, although you can have as many child forms as you wish. Delphi does not prevent you from creating more than one MDI parent form, but the application will give an error message when you try to compile it.

Displaying child forms

It is surprising that when you run this application, the child forms are automatically displayed. When you start a new project, the main form is inserted into the list of auto-create forms. When a child window is added to a project it is also added to this list. To prevent this happening remove the child forms from the list using the **Project | Options** menu as shown in fig 7.20.

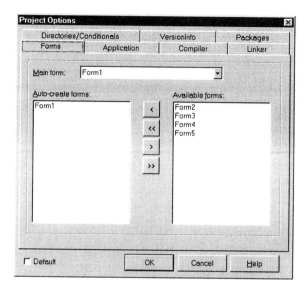

Fig 7.20 *Auto-creation of forms.*

When you have done this the child forms will not be automatically displayed. To show these forms you cannot simply use the *Show* method, you need to instantiate the forms using the *Create* method, you can then use the **Show** method:

> *Form2 := TForm2.Create(Self);*
> *Form2.Show;*

This code and some interesting attributes can be demonstrated by a small application:

- Start a new application.
- Change the **FormStyle** property so that *Form1* is a parent form.
- Add a new form.
- Change the **FormStyle** property of *Form2* so that it is a child form.
- Remove *Form2* from the list of auto-created forms.
- Add a button to the parent form and add the two lines of code for creating and showing *Form2*.

When you run this application and click on the button, as expected *Form2* is displayed within *Form1*. What may be more surprising is that every time you click on the button another instance of *Form2* is created. Every form you create is a new instance of the class *TForm2*. Classes and instances are covered in chapter 9.

Closing child forms

When you close a child form, it is minimised and appears at the bottom of the parent form. You can control this by changing the value of the **Action** parameter in the **OnClose** event for the window. This parameter can have the following values:

*Table 7.4 The **Action** parameter in the **OnClose** event.*

Value	Meaning
caNone	The form cannot close.
caHide	The form is hidden, not closed, and is still available to the application.
caFree	The form is closed and all the resources it is using are given up.
caMinimize	The default for child forms. The form is minimised.

When the parent window is minimised all of the child windows are also minimised. When the parent is closed all the child windows are closed.

Arranging forms

There are three key methods which you can use for arranging forms:

- The **Cascade** method arranges the forms in an overlapping way.
- The **Tile** method arranges forms so that they are not overlapping. You can control how they are displayed by setting the **TileMode** property to **tbVertical** or **tbHorizontal,** prior to calling **Tile**. The **TileMode** property does not function correctly as described in the on-line help.
- The **ArrangeIcons** method arranges minimised forms neatly at the bottom of the parent form.

The Object Repository

Sometimes when you have created a form you want to be able to use it in another application. You can do this for forms and other objects using the Object Repository.

To add a form to the Object Repository, select the form and click on the right mouse button to display the speed-menu. The dialog shown in fig 7.21 is displayed.

The list of pages available corresponds to the pages you see when you choose the **File | New** Option. If you add a form to the Form page Object repository, you will see that it has been added to that page and can be added to another project.

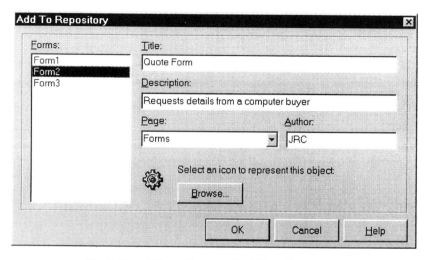

Fig 7.21 Adding a form to the Object Repository.

You can add new pages to the repository by using the **Tools | Repository** menu option. This dialog is shown in fig 7.22.

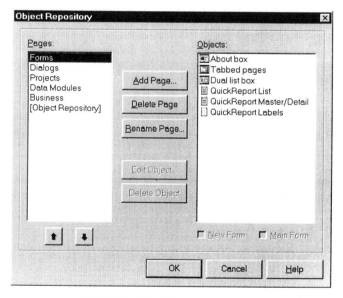

Fig 7.22 The Object Repository.

8

Object Pascal

Introduction

One of the great things about Delphi is that you can develop a lot of your applications without writing very much Object Pascal code. In the examples we have seen so far, we have only had to write a few lines of code, however if you want to develop powerful applications you do need to have a good understanding of Object Pascal. If you are already a Pascal programmer it is worthwhile reading this chapter, since there are many variants of the language, each with its own features. If you have programmed using languages such as 'C' but do not know Pascal well, you should find the transition easy. If you are a new programmer, this chapter has all you need to develop serious applications.

The special features of Object Pascal related to the object orientation aspects of the language and how it differs from 'standard' Pascal are covered in the next chapter.

In this chapter you will learn about:

- Standard data types.
- Procedures and functions.
- Assignment statements.
- Controlling program flow.

Standard data types

Object Pascal code has two main components, the code statements and the data. The code statements perform operations of the data. We have already used both of these implicitly, but now we need to look in more detail at how data is used. All the data items that you use are a specific named type. These different types have different sizes and can store a different range of values. Object Pascal offers a wide range of standard data types and also allows you to define your own. The most common groups of data types are integers and floating point. There are several forms of these types of variables. The integer types are shown in table 8.1. All sizes are in bytes.

Table 8.1 *Integer data types.*

Data Type	Size	Range
Integer	2	-32768 → 32767.
Shortint	1	-128 → 127.
Longint	4	-2147483647 → 2147483647.
Byte	1	0 → 255.
Word	2	0 – 65535.
Cardinal	2	0 → 65535.

The floating point types are listed in table 8.2. The **Real** type should be avoided, since it is only included for compatibility with version 1 of Delphi.

Table 8.2 *Floating point data types.*

Data Type	Size	Description
Single	4	7→8 significant digits in the fractional part.
Double	8	15→16 significant digits.
Extended	10	19→20 significant digits.
Real	6	11→12 significant digits.
Comp	8	1929 significant digits.
Currency	8	High-precision real number stored in integer format, with 4 decimal places.

Table 8.3 *Miscellaneous data types.*

Data Type	Size	Description
Boolean	1	True or False.
AnsiChar	1	An ANSI character.
Char	1	Same as ANSI Char.
WideChar	1	A Unicode character.
ShortString	varies	A sequence of up to 255 characters.
AnsiString	varies	A dynamic string of any size.
String	varies	By default the same as **AnsiString**.
Variant	16	This data type can hold values of any type and can convert between types as required.
String	0→255	A list of characters.
Pointer	2	A pointer to an unspecified type.
PChar	2	A pointer to a null-terminated string.

The remaining data types are listed in table 8.3.

Declaring variables

Identifiers are the names of variables, functions, procedures, methods and so on which are used in an application. In Object Pascal, before an identifier is used, it must be declared. When you declare an identifier you must declare its name and also its type in the **var** section of the unit, for example:

```
procedure TForm1.Button1Click(Sender: TObject);
var
    memorySize, diskSize : Integer;
    description : String;
    cost: String;
```

If you have more than one variable of a type to declare, you can put them on the same line, separated by commas:

Put the variable declaration of variable after the start of the procedure and before the start of the executable program.

Declaring constants

Sometimes you want to create an identifier which will not change, that is a constant. It is a good idea to use constants rather than "hard-coding" numbers into your code. If you have used a particular value throughout your application it is best to declare that this value is a constant. If you change the value of the constant, the new value is used whenever you compile. You have already seen constants used extensively, for example to make a child form set the form's **FormStyle** property equal to the constant **fsMDIChild**.

To declare a constant the keyword **const** is used, for example:

```
const
    MemoryCost = 200;
    CpuCost = 500;
    TotalCost = MemoryCost + CpuCost;
    supplierName = 'Mega Systems';
```

The keyword **const** is followed by the name of the constant and its value. You can have mathematical expressions that can be calculated at compile time.

Converting between types

If you are used to programming in Visual Basic, Delphi will seem very fussy about how its variables and constants can be used. If you assign one identifier to another, the two must be of the same type. If they are not, you need to use a function to carry out a conversion. The main functions are given in table 8.4.

Table 8.4 *Converting between data types.*

Function name	Description
IntToStr	Integer to string.
StrToInt	String to integer.
IntToHex	Integer to string in hexadecimal format.
HexToStr	Hexadecimal number to string.
FloatToStr	Float to String with 15 significant digits.
StrToFloat	String to float.
StrToCurr	String to Currency.
CurrToStr	Currency to string.
StrToDate	String to date.
DateToStr	Date to string.
StrToTime	String to time.
TimeToStr	Time to string.

The time and date functions return the current time and date. If you want to display either of these, for example, in a label, you must convert them to a string:

> *Label1.Caption := DateToStr(Date);*
> *Label2.Caption := TimeToStr(Time);*

FloatToStr is the most commonly used function for converting between floating point and string formats, but you can use the **FloatToStrF** function, which gives you much more control over how the string is produced. There are three parameters in place of the usual one:

- The value to be converted is the first parameter.
- The *format* parameter is the second value. The possible options are given in table 8.5.
- The final parameter is in two parts, *precision* which is the maximum number of digits in the string, and *digits* which specifies the number of digits after the decimal point or the minimum number after the exponent if the scientific number format is used.

The format parameter can have the following values:

Table 8.5 *Values of the format parameter.*

Value	Description
ffGeneral	General number format. If the number is less than 0.00001, the scientific format is used and the Digits parameter gives the minimum number of digits in the exponent, between 0 and 4.
ffExponent	Scientific number format. Digits gives the minimum number of parameters in the exponent, between 0 and 4.
ffFixed	Fixed point format. The number of digits after the decimal point is given by the third parameter, Digits gives the number of digits after the decimal point, between 0 and 18.
ffNumber	The same as **ffFixed** except a thousands separator is used.
ffCurrency	The format is controlled by the Regional Settings option of the Windows Control Panel. Digits gives the number of digits after the decimal point, between 0 and 18.

The code shown below displays the same number using each of the different formats, each one giving a different string:

```
procedure TForm1.Button1Click(Sender: TObject);
const
v =123456789.87654321;
begin
memo1.Lines[0] := 'ffGeneral' + FloatToStrF(v,ffgeneral,10,2);
memo1.Lines[1] :='ffExponent' FloatToStrF(v,ffExponent,10,2);
memo1.Lines[2] :='fffixed ' + FloatToStrF(v,ffFixed,10,2);
memo1.Lines[3] := 'ffNumber ' + FloatToStrF(v,ffNumber,10,2);
memo1.Lines[4] :='ffCurrency'+ FloatToStrF(v,ffCurrency,10,2);
end;
```

The running application is shown in fig 8.1.

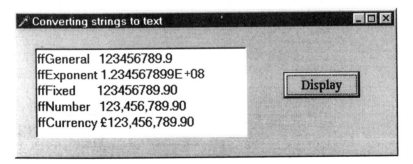

Fig 8.1 *Using the **FloatToStrF** function.*

Operators

When you have declared all the data you want to use, operators allow you to manipulate that data. Object Pascal has a full complement of operators for:

- Arithmetic.
- Comparison.
- Logical operations.
- Bitwise operations.

There are six arithmetic operators are shown in table 8.6.

Table 8.6 *The arithmetic operators.*

Operator	Description
+	Add.
-	Subtract.
*	Multiply.
/	Divide.
div	Integer division.
mod	The remainder after dividing two integers.

The standard set of relational and assignment operators is provided:

Table 8.7 *The relational operators.*

Operator	Description
:=	Assignment.
=	Test for equality.
>	Greater than.
>=	Greater than or equal to.
<	Less than.
<=	Less than or equal to.
<>	Not equal.

It is a common mistake to confuse the '=' and ':=' operators. If you want to test for equality between two identifiers use '=', if you want to do an assignment use ':='. For example:

*if age = 17 **then** message := 'Too young to vote';*

These operators can be used on strings as well as numerical values.

Object Pascal also has the usual set of logical or boolean operators shown in table 8.8.

Table 8.8 _The logical operators._

Operator	Description
not	Negation.
and	Logical and.
or	Logical or.
xor	Logical exclusive or.

Unlike the other logical operator **not** is applied to only one boolean identifier, for example:

```
var
    Ok : Boolean
begin
    Ok := CheckReadyStatus;
    if (not Ok) then ShowMessage('Not ready');
end;
```

The boolean _Ok_ is returned by the procedure _CheckReadyStatus_. If a value of False is returned, the value of _**not** Ok_ is True and the message box is displayed.

The **and** operator checks to see if both of the supplied values are True; if they are then a value of True is generated.

```
if (memory <= 16) and (processorSpeed < 120) then
    ShowMessage('Not ideal for Windows 95');
```

In this code fragment, if the memory size is less than or equal to 16Mb **and** the processor speed is less than 120MHz, then this is not an ideal machine for Windows 95.

The inclusive or: **or** and the exclusive or: **xor** are very similar. If you use the **or** operator , then if either of the values is true or both are True a value of True is returned. If you use the **xor** operator, then a value of True is returned if either of the values is True but not if both are True.

```
if (age < 25) or (engineSize >2000) then
begin
    ShowMessage('Extra car insurance premium');
end;
```

It is correct to use **or** in this example, if the age of the car driver is under 25 or the engine size is over 2000cc, or if both of these conditions are True then there is an extra insurance premium. If you used **xor** in this case, drivers who are both under 25 and have cars with large engines would not be charged a higher premium.

Bitwise operators

Object Pascal has six bitwise operators which operate directly on the bit patterns of the variables.

Table 8.9 *The bitwise operators.*

Operator	Description
not	Bitwise negation.
and	Bitwise and.
or	Bitwise inclusive or.
xor	Bitwise exclusive or.
shl	Bitwise shift left.
shr	Bitwise shift right.

Controlling program flow

We have already looked implicitly at the **if** statement as a way of controlling program flow. We are going to look at this in more detail and also at the other ways in which you can control program flow. There are two branching statements in Object Pascal:

- **if then else**.
- **case** .

and three looping statements

- **repeat**.
- **while**.
- **for**.

If then else statements

It can be difficult to see how these statements are used without an example to look at. The form shown in fig 8.2 requests some information prior to quoting for the cost of motorbike insurance. When you click on exit, a dialog is displayed indicating if there is a problem, for example drivers with a drink driving conviction are not insurable. When you select a particular make of bike, a dialog is displayed telling you if there is a discount or premium on bikes of this type.

The components are given meaningful names in this application. The text box with the age is called *driverAge*. The drink driving checkbox is called *drunk* and the reckless driving checkbox is called *reckless*. The insurance radio group is called *insurance*. The list box of manufacturers is called *manufacturer*.

Some code is added to the **OnClick** event procedure for the *Exit* button to ensure that some conditions are met or to display some information.

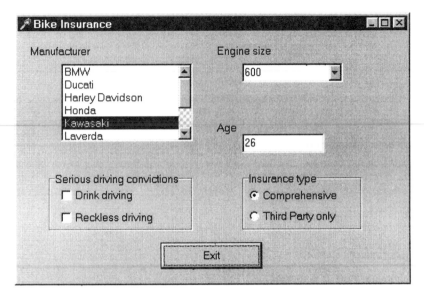

Fig 8.2 *The bike insurance quote form.*

In the **OnClick** event procedure, a string called *m* is defined, this contains the text which is displayed on clicking the exit button. An integer variable *age* is also defined and this is assigned to the value of *StrToInt(driverAge.Text)*, that is the integer form of the text in the *age* text box.

```
procedure TForm1.exitButtonClick(Sender: TObject);
var
    m: String;
    age : Integer;
begin
    m := '';
    age := StrToInt(driverAge.Text);
    if age < 17 then m := 'Too young to drive';
    ... ...
```

If the driver specifies an age of less than 17, the text which is displayed in the dialog is *'Too young to drive'*, (in England). If you wish to extend this so that drivers over 75 cannot drive, you can amend the line to include an **else** clause:

```
if age < 17 then m := 'Too young to drive' else
    If (age > 75) then m := 'To old to drive';
```

If the driver has a conviction for drink driving or for reckless driving then they are uninsurable by this company. The following line of code must be added which tests for these two conditions:

```
if (reckless.Checked = true) or (drunk.Checked = true) then
    m := 'Sorry, we cannot insure you with this conviction';
```

You can also use nested if clauses:

```
if (age >= 17) then
begin
    if (age < 25) then
    begin
        if (insurance.ItemIndex = 0) then
            m := 'Sorry we cannot insure you comprehensively';
    end;
end;
```

These statements assign the text shown to *m* if the driver is between 17 and 24. To display the message dialog add the following lines:

```
if m <> '' then MessageDlg(m, mtInformation,[mbOk],0);
```

An example of the dialog produced is shown in fig 8.3.

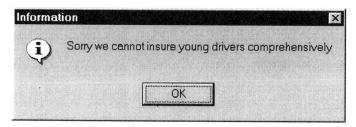

Fig 8.3 *The warning dialog.*

Case statements

When you select a particular manufacturer, a dialog is displayed indicating if there is a discount or extra premium on bikes of this type. The code to do this is in the click event for the *manufacturer* list box. This can be written using **if** statements:

```
procedure TForm1.manufacturerClick(Sender: TObject);
var
    m : String;
    c : Integer;
begin
    c := manufacturer.ItemIndex;
    m := 'Sorry no discount';
    if c = 0 then m := 'There is a 15% discount on BMW bikes';
    if c = 2 then m :='We offer a 25% discount on Harleys';
    if (c = 1) or (c = 5) then
        m:= 'There is a 10% extra premium on Italian bikes';
    if (c = 3) or (c = 4) or (c = 6) or (c=7) then
```

```
        m := 'We offer a 10% discount on Japanese bikes';
     MessageDlg(m, mtInformation,[mbOk],0);
end;
```

An alternative way of coding this is to use the case statement:

```
case c of
     0: m := 'There is a 15% discount on BMW bikes';
     2: m :='We offer a 25% discount on insuring Harleys';
     1,5 : m:= 'There is a 10% extra premium on Italian bikes';
     3,4,6,7 : m := 'We offer a 10% discount on Japanese bikes';
else
     m := 'Sorry no discount';
end;
     MessageDlg(m, mtInformation,[mbOk],0);
```

A typical dialog produced by this code is shown in fig 8.4.

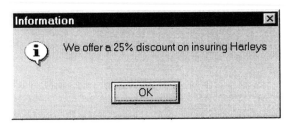

Fig 8.4 *Displaying discount rates.*

The only drawback is that the identifier used (in this case *m*) can only be either an integer (but not **Longint**), a char or an enumerated type. Enumerated types are covered later.

Repeat statements

The **repeat** instruction allows a set of instructions to be repeated until a condition is met. Fig 8.5 shows a **StringGrid** component with the column and row of each cell displayed. You could add the text to the cells using a line of code for each cell, but it is much easier to do so using the looping constructs of Object Pascal.

The code required is added to the **FormCreate** event. Firstly to add the text to the first row in the grid:

```
procedure TForm1.FormCreate(Sender: TObject);
var
     c ,r : Integer;
begin
     StringGrid1.RowCount := 5;
     StringGrid1.ColCount := 5;
```

```
c := -1;
r := 0;
repeat
    c := c + 1;
    StringGrid1.Cells[c, r] := IntToStr(c)+ ',' + IntToStr(r);
until c = StringGrid1.ColCount;
end;
```

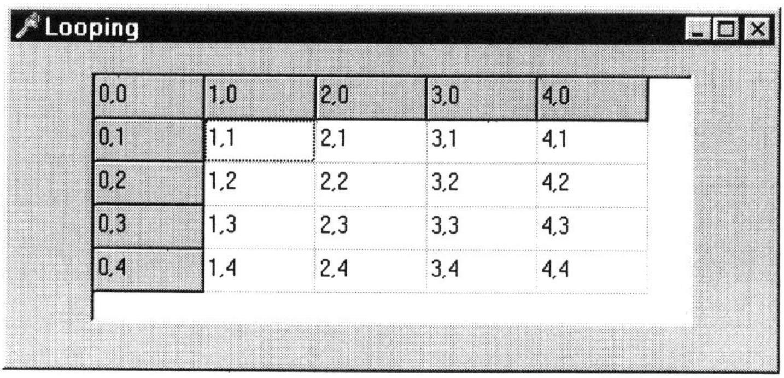

Fig 8.5 *The **repeat until** statement.*

The **RowCount** and **ColCount** properties of the **StringGrid** component specifies the number of rows and columns in the grid. The text within a particular cell is given by the **Cells** property.

The code within the **repeat until** loop is repeated until the condition specified at the **until** clause is met, in this case when the variable c is equal to the number of columns.

If you want to add the text for the remaining rows, the body of this procedure has to be modified as shown:

```
begin
StringGrid1.RowCount := 5;
StringGrid1.ColCount := 5;
c := -1;
r := -1;
repeat
    c := c + 1;
    repeat
        r := r + 1;
        StringGrid1.Cells[c, r] := IntToStr(c)+ ',' + IntToStr(r);
    until r = StringGrid1.RowCount;
    r := -1;
until c = StringGrid1.ColCount;
end;
```

This code produces the form shown in fig 8.5.

While statements

While statements are similar to **repeat** statements except that the terminating condition is checked at the start - so the statements within the **while** block may not execute even once the termination condition is met. The code below produces exactly the same output as the **repeat until** loop in the previous example.

```
procedure TForm1.FormCreate(Sender: TObject);
var
c, r : Integer;
begin
StringGrid1.RowCount := 5;
StringGrid1.ColCount := 5;
c := -1;
r := -1;
while c < StringGrid1.ColCount do
    begin
    c := c + 1;
    while r < StringGrid1.RowCount do
        begin
        r := r + 1;
        StringGrid1.Cells[c, r] := IntToStr(c)+ ',' + IntToStr(r);
        end;
    r := -1;
    end;
end;
```

The key differences to note are that the test for termination of the loop is specified at the start, rather than the end. The **begin end** pair determines what is within the **while** loop.

For statements

If you want to increase a value every time a looping value is executed, you can use a **for** statement. The code below does the same as the two previous examples, but is much more streamlined:

```
procedure TForm1.FormCreate(Sender: TObject);
var
c, r : Integer;
begin
StringGrid1.RowCount := 5;
StringGrid1.ColCount := 5;
for c := 0 to StringGrid1.Colcount do
    begin
```

```
    for r := 0 to StringGrid1.RowCount do
        StringGrid1.Cells[c, r] := IntToStr(c)+ ',' + IntToStr(r);
    end;
end;
```

The first **for** loop assigns the variable c to 0. The code within the **begin end** pair constitutes the code which is within the block. The second time this block is executed, c is increased to 1 and so on, until the value of *c* is greater than *StringGrid1.ColCount.*

The second loop gives *r* an initial value of r and increases it every time the loop is executed until it is greater than *StringGrid1.RowCount.* Note that there is only one line within this **for** loop and so it does not need to be enclosed within a **begin end** pair.

The **for** loop can count down as well as up, by using the key word **downto**, for example:

```
    for c :=10 downto 0 do
        grid[c] := c;
```

The first time the loop is executed c has the value 10, the next, a value of 9 and so on, down 0.

Calling procedures and functions

All of the code we have written so far has gone into an event procedure, but you can create your own procedures so that you do not have to write the same code repeatedly. Often applications only want an integer value to be input into a text box, if for example a disk or memory size is being specified. You can put the code used to check if an integer has been input into a procedure and call that procedure rather than repeating the code many times. The *CheckForInteger* procedure carries out this check:

```
    procedure CheckForInteger(s: String);
    var
        i, pos: Integer;
        m : Integer
    begin
        Val(s, i, pos);
        if (pos <> 0) and (s <> '') then
        begin
            m :='Must be an integer try again';
            MessageDlg(m, mtWarning, [mbOk], 0);
        end;
    end;
```

The procedure **Val** has three parameters:

- The parameter *s* is a string which is to be converted to its numeric representation.
- The second parameter *i* is the numeric representation of the string.

- The third parameter indicates if an error has occurred. If there is no error *pos* is zero. If an invalid, non-integer character is found, *pos* gives the position in the string of that character (if the first character is in error, 1 is returned and so on.)

An application which uses this procedure is shown in fig 8.6. The application requests integer values to be specified for the memory size and CD speed. If a non-integer value is input, as is the case for the memory size, the warning message is displayed.

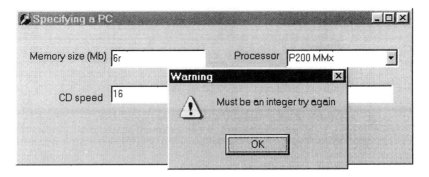

Fig 8.6 Using procedures.

The edit box used for the memory size is called *edit1*. To perform the validation check the *CheckForInteger* procedure is called as shown in the code below:

```
procedure TForm1.Edit1Change(Sender: TObject);
begin
      CheckForInteger(Edit1.Text);
end;
```

The same line of code is inserted in the change event handlers for all of the edit boxes which expect only integers. The *CheckForInteger* procedure must be placed before the procedure which calls it in the unit file.

Passing by value and address

In the previous example a single parameter was passed to the procedure. Sometimes you will want to pass more than one parameter and you may also wish to change the value of one of the parameters and pass it back to the calling procedure. A procedure for calculating the average of three numbers would look like the one shown below:

```
procedure GetAverage(var av: Single, val1, val2, val3 : Single)
begin
      av := (val1 + val2 + val3)/3;
end;
```

```
procedure MyProcedure
var
    average, value1, value2, value3 : Single;
begin
    value1 := 2.3;
    value1 := 7.3;
    value3 := 8.9;
    GetAverage (average, value1, value2, value3);
    Edit1.Text := FloatToStr(average);;
end;
```

In this code the three identifiers *val1*, *val2* and val3 remain unchanged, while the identifier *av* is changed in the called procedure and the result passed back.

val1, *val2* and *val3* are passed by value, that is a copy of the current value of the identifier is passed to the called routine. The first parameter is passed by address, and can be changed in the called procedure. It is preceded by the keyword **var** in the called procedure.

Note that the names of the parameters in the calling and called procedures do not have to be the same. The first parameter in the calling list refers to the first parameter in the called routine and so on.

Using functions

It is rather clumsy passing a variable to a procedure so that it can be changed and passed back, and sometimes it is better to call a function rather than a procedure.

```
function GetAverage( val1, val2, val3 : Single) : Single
begin
    GetAverage := (val1 + val2 + val3)/3;
end;

procedure MyProcedure
var
    average, value1, value2, value3 : Single;
begin
    average := GetAverage( value1, value2, value3);
    edit1.Text := FloatToStr(average);
end;
```

The differences between the function and procedure *GetAverage* are:

- The reserved word **procedure** is replaced by **function**.
- The function type is declared as **single**. This dictates the type of the returned value.
- The function name *GetAverage* is assigned to the value to be returned. This value is available in the calling routine.

- In the calling procedure, the call to the function forms the right hand side of an assignment statement.

When you wish to return a single value, you should use a function.

9

Creating Records, Classes and Objects

Introduction

We have covered enough Object Pascal to allow you to create powerful applications, but there are some additional features that we have not yet looked at. In particular we have not looked at how you can create your own data types or how you use the object aspects of the language. If you are new to object orientation it can seem tricky to understand the key concepts and to use them. Object orientation has now become the most accepted way of designing and writing software and if you choose not to think and program using this approach you will find it hard to follow many of the current trends, particularly if you are interested in learning languages such as Java.

In this chapter you will learn how to:

- Define your own data types.
- Create and use records.
- Create classes.
- Instantiate objects.

Defining data types

In addition to the standard data types Object Pascal allows you to define your own data types. The main categories of user defined data types are:

- Enumerated types.
- Sub-range types.
- Arrays.
- Records.

Enumerated types

An enumerated type lists all the possible values that a variable of that type can have, for example:

```
type
    TWeekDays = (Monday, Tuesday, Wednesday, Thursday, Friday);
    TWeekend = (Saturday, Sunday);
```

These statements define two data types of type *TweekDays* and *Tweekend*. They both start with a capital *T* to indicate that they are types; this is not compulsory but it is a useful convention to use. Before you can use these types, you need to create some identifiers of these types, in the same way that you need to create identifiers of standard types such as **integer** and **single** before using them:

```
var
    day : TweekDays;
```

You can then make assignments or tests using the declared variable:

```
today := Tuesday;
if (day = Monday) then StartOfWeek( );
```

Underlying these enumerated types are an integer data structure, but it is easier to use enumerated types to give meaningful names such as the days of the week rather than using the alternative:

```
var
    day : integer;
begin
    day := 2;
    if (day = 1) then StartOfWeek ( );
```

Enumerated types can be very useful, particularly when you are using radio buttons to specify your choice as shown in fig 9.1.

If you choose a Pentium or Pentium MMX processor the preferred operating system is Windows 95. If you have a Pentium II, Windows NT is the usual choice. The application shown in fig 9.1 changes the type of operating system displayed depending on which processor you choose. The code required is shown:

```
type
TProcessor = (P166, P200, P200MMX, PII233, PII266);

procedure TForm1.RadioGroup1Click(Sender: TObject);
var
mp : TProcessor;
begin
case RadioGroup1.ItemIndex of
    0 : mp := P166;
```

```
1 : mp := P200;
2 : mp := P200MMX;
3 : mp := PII233;
4 : mp := PII266;
end;
if (mp =PII233) or (mp = PII266) then edit1.Text:='Windows NT'
else edit1.Text := 'Windows 95';
end;
```

The type follows the convention of starting with the letter *T*.

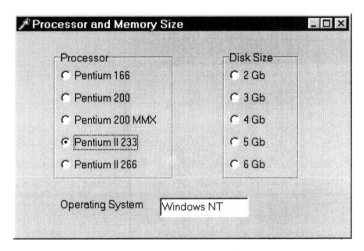

Fig 9.1 *Using enumerated types.*

Sub-range types

Sub-range types allow you to limit the range of an existing integer, char, boolean or enumerated type. For example, if your application is asking how many hours you worked yesterday it expects a number between 1 and 24 hours. (It just feels like more sometimes!)

```
Type
    THoursWorked = 0..24;
    TLowerCase = 'a'..'z';
    TProcessor = (80386, 80486, Pentium, PentiumII);
    TProcessorsFor95 = 80386..Pentium;
```

Thours is an integer type with a value between 0 and 24, and *TLowerCase* is a character between 'a' and 'z'. *Tprocessors* is a definition of an enumerated type of a list of processors. *TProcessorsFor95* is a list of the processors from the *80386* through to *Pentium*.

Arrays

An array is a set of data items of the same type. If you want to save a list of values an array is an ideal choice, for example, to save a list of costs:

var
    costs : **array[1..5] of Single**;

This defines a one-dimensional array with 5 elements, the first element is referred to as *costs[1]*, and the last as *costs[5]*. These array elements are used in the same way as other identifiers. The benefit of having them in an array is that they can be referred to very easily using looping constructs:

    sum := 0;
    for *count =1* ***to 5 do***
        sum := sum + cost[count];

A special type of one dimensional array is used for storing strings, for example:

    Names : **string[10]**;

This creates a string of 10 characters.

Arrays can have many dimensions, but the most useful ones have either one or two dimensions, for example:

var
    myTable : **array [1..5, 1..5] of Integer**;

This can be especially useful when accessing a grid. The **Cells** property of a grid contains the contents of the cells. Rows and columns are both numbered from 0 upwards, with the top left corner as the 0,0 position. The grid shown has been used to display information about animals in a zoo.

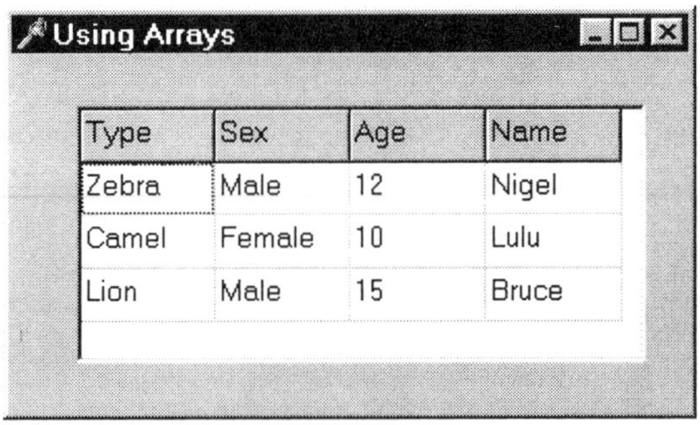

Type	Sex	Age	Name
Zebra	Male	12	Nigel
Camel	Female	10	Lulu
Lion	Male	15	Bruce

Fig 9.2 Using grids.

The individual cells can be loaded at run-time, in the form create event as follows:

    procedure *TForm1.FormCreate(Sender: TObject);*
    begin

```
      StringGrid1.RowCount := 4;
      StringGrid1.ColCount := 4;
      StringGrid1.Fixedcols := 0;
      StringGrid1.Cells[0,0] := 'Type';
      StringGrid1.Cells[1,0] := 'Sex';
      StringGrid1.Cells[2,0] := 'Age';
      StringGrid1.Cells[3,0] := 'Name';
      StringGrid1.Cells[0,1] := 'Zebra';
      StringGrid1.Cells[1,1] := 'Male';
      StringGrid1.Cells[2,1] := '12';
      StringGrid1.Cells[3,1] := 'Nigel';
      StringGrid1.Cells[0,2] := 'Camel';
      StringGrid1.Cells[1,2] := 'Female';
      StringGrid1.Cells[2,2] := '10';
      StringGrid1.Cells[3,2] := 'Lulu';
      StringGrid1.Cells[0,3] := 'Lion';
      StringGrid1.Cells[1,3] := 'Male';
      StringGrid1.Cells[2,3] := '15';
      StringGrid1.Cells[3,3] := 'Bruce';
  end;
```

The **RowCount** property of the grid gives the number of rows (the **ColCount** property gives the number of columns). The number of fixed columns and rows is given by **FixedCols** and **FixedRows**.

Records

A record is a collection of items of data which may be of different types. For example, you may wish to create a record which contains details of the animals in the zoo:

```
type
      TGender = (Male, Female);

type
      TAnimal = record
          animalType : String[10];
          sex : Tgender;
          age : Integer;
          name : String[10];
      end;
```

You can now create data items of type *TAnimal*:

```
var
      zebra, lion : TAnimal;
```

Note that the record created contains a data item which is an enumerated type, representing the gender. You can refer to individual elements of the identifier *zebra*, for example:

```
zebra.animalType := 'Zebra';
zebra.sex :=Male;
zebra.age := 12;
zebra.name := 'Nigel';
```

Specify the name of the identifier, followed by the name of the component you want to refer to. A useful shorthand way of assigning values is to use the **with** statement:

```
with lion do
    begin
        animalType := 'Lion';
        sex := Male;
        age := 15;
        name := 'Bruce';
    end;
```

Delphi has a very flexible programming language, with a wide range of data types and strong data type checking which is invaluable in reducing bugs. In addition to this it also has a strong object orientated aspect. Some Delphi programmers choose to ignore the object orientation of Delphi and use it as if it is a visual Pascal, but it is worth spending time finding out about object orientation, since it does help you to write bug free Windows applications faster, which is what Delphi is all about.

Why bother with object orientation?

You can write successful applications without explicitly using object orientation, but if you choose to do so you are missing out on one of the biggest revolutions in software design in the past decade. Object orientation is a new way of designing software which allows you to model real-world situations easier than any other technique. Delphi, unlike languages such as Visual Basic, it is a true object oriented environment which has all of the language elements needed to allow you to implement an object orientated design. Object orientation allows you to construct your software from re-usable components or objects, which makes it easier to write less error prone software with the minimum of effort.

Classes and Objects

We have already been using classes and objects extensively. Every one of the components we have used is an object and a member of a defined class. If, for example, you add buttons to a form, the buttons are all members of the same class, in this case **TButton**. Each button is an object, the first has the default name *Button1* and so on. The class has a number of properties associated with it, in the case of the **TButton** class the properties are **Cancel**, **Caption**, and so on as shown in fig 9.3.

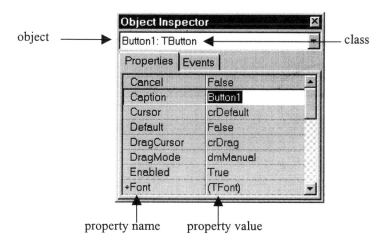

Fig 9.3 Objects and classes.

Since *Button1* is an object which is a member of the **TButton** class it has all of the properties of that class. In object orientation jargon *Button1* is an instance of **TButton**. Every time that you place a component on a form you create an object, which is an instance of the relevant component class.

At this point it may seem that a class is no different from the definition of the record structure described earlier, since both define a new type which contains a set of data items. One of the key differences is that classes also have a set of procedures associated with them called methods, for example the **TButton** class supports the **OnClick** event, the **OnDragDrop** event and so on.

The class defines the behaviour and properties. Objects are instances of a class and the way they behave is determined by the class to which they belong. It is crucial to understand the differences between a class and an object to use object orientation.

Using properties and methods

We have already implicitly used the properties and methods of the visual objects in Delphi extensively. To refer to the property of an object, specify the name of the object, a period, and the name of the property, for example:

*Text1.**Text** := 'Buy more memory!';*

The name of the object is *Text1* and the property is **Text**.

Similarly if you wish to use the method of a object, specify the object name, a period, and the method name, for example:

*Form1.**Show**;*

The name of the object is *Form1* and the method name is **Show**.

Creating classes

In addition to using the pre-defined visual classes in Delphi, you can create and use your own. In this section we are going to look at the structure of the unit file and how you create a new class with three methods. The running application we are going to develop is shown in fig 9.4.

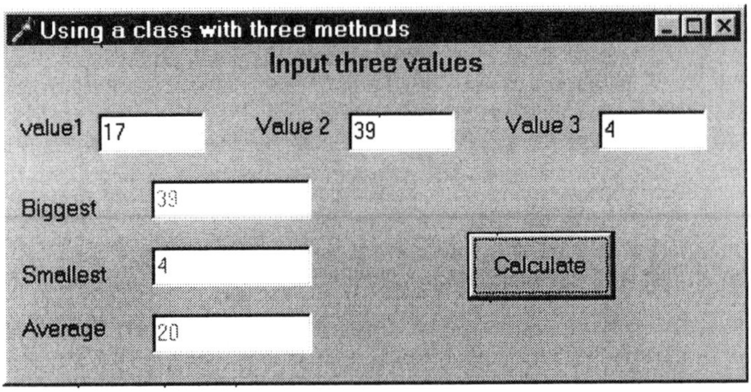

Fig 9.4 The running application.

Three integer values are entered into the top three text boxes. When the button is clicked the biggest, the smallest and the average of the values are presented. These three text boxes have their **Enabled** property set to False so that they cannot be altered at run-time by the application user.

Most of the top of the unit file is created for you by Delphi, but it is good to know a little more about it. In the unit file shown below, the reserved word **unit** is followed by the name of the unit file, in this case *Unit1*. The **interface** reserved word is followed by the **uses** clause which lists unit files which are used by this unit.

> *unit Unit1;*
> *interface*
> *uses*
> *Windows, Messages, SysUtils, Classes, Graphics, Controls,*
> *Forms, Dialogs, StdCtrls;*

The **type** reserved word marks the start of the definition of a new class. The name of the new class is *TForm1* and is based on a standard windows class called **TForm**. This new class contains an object called *Button1* which is of class **TButton**, an object called *Edit1* of class **TEdit** and so on. This class has two methods associated with it, *Button1Click*, the **OnClick** event handler for the *Button1* object and *FormCreate*, the **OnFormCreate** event handler.

```
type
TForm1 = class(TForm)
    Button1: TButton;
    Edit1: TEdit;
    Edit2: TEdit;
    Edit3: TEdit;
    Edit4: TEdit;
    Edit5: TEdit;
    Label1: TLabel;
    Label2: TLabel;
    Edit6: TEdit;
    Label3: TLabel;
    Label4: TLabel;
    Label5: TLabel;
    Label6: TLabel;
    Label7: TLabel;
    procedure Button1Click(Sender: TObject);
    procedure FormCreate(Sender: TObject);
```

To add our own class and methods using the same notation:

```
TCalculate = class(TObject)
    Function Big(v1,v2, v3 : String) : String;
    Function Small(v1, v2, v3 : String) : String;
    Function Average(v1, v2, v3 : String) : String;
end;
var
    Form1: TForm1;
    a : TCalculate;
```

The *TCalculate* class is based on the **TObject** class (all the classes you create are based on this class). This class contains only three methods, the three functions *Big*, *Small* and *Average*. Each of these functions has three parameters, *v1*, *v2* and *v3* all are strings. The returned value is of type **string**.

In the **var** section Delphi will automatically define the object *Form1* as being of type *TForm1*. We need to add the line defining the object *a* as being of type *TCalculate*. We have now defined the *TCalculate* class and defined an instance of it. The next stage is to write the code for the click event handler for *Button1*. You can use this class in exactly the same way as one of the standard classes:

```
procedure TForm1.Button1Click(Sender: TObject);
begin
    Edit4.Text:=a.Big(Edit1.Text, Edit2.Text, Edit3.Text);
    Edit5.Text :=a.Small(Edit1.Text, Edit2.Text, Edit3.Text);
    Edit6.Text:=a.Average(Edit1.Text, Edit2.Text, Edit3.Text);
end;
```

The *Big* method for the object called *a* can be referred to by specifying the name of the object (*a*), by the name of the method (*Big*) and the parameters it requires. Similarly you can use the *Smallest* and *Average* methods.

Finally we need to actually write these methods, the code for them is shown below:

```
function TCalculate.Big(v1,v2,v3 : String) : String;
var
    intResult : Integer;
begin
    intResult := StrToInt(v1);
    if (StrToInt(v2) > intResult) then intResult := StrToInt(v2);
    if (StrToInt(v3) > intResult) then intResult := StrToInt(v3);
    result := IntToStr(intResult);
end;

function TCalculate.Smallest(v1,v2,v3 : String) : String;
var
    intResult : Integer;
begin
    intResult := StrToInt(v1);
    if (StrToInt(v2) < intResult) then intResult := StrToInt(v2);
    if (StrToInt(v3) < intResult) then intResult := StrToInt(v3);
    result := IntToStr(intResult);
end;

function TCalculate.Average(v1,v2,v3 : String) : String;
var
    intResult : Integer;
begin
    intResult := (StrToInt(v1)+StrToInt(v2)+StrToInt(v3)) div 3;
    result := IntToStr(intResult);
end;
```

It may not seem as if there is any saving in creating and using these classes, but you can use them repeatedly throughout your applications without the need to rewrite the same code.

10
Creating Active Forms

Introduction

The growth of the Internet has been one of the greatest success stories in the history of computing. There are currently nearly 100 million Internet users world-wide and the numbers are doubling every year. The Internet allows people to access information anywhere in the world for the cost of a local phone call. The Internet is a network of computers which communicates through a protocol called TCP/IP (Transmission Control Protocol / Internet Protocol). One of the most important parts of the Internet is the World Wide Web, which uses the infrastructure of the Internet for data transfer. The World Wide Web uses mainly HTTP (HyperText Transfer Protocol) and FTP (File Transfer Protocol) to communicate between the WWW server and the user. The user needs a browser which is capable of understanding these protocols. What this means is that information placed on a WWW server anywhere in the world can be viewed by any Internet user who has a browser which can understand HTTP and FTP.

Delphi uses ActiveX technology to allow you to create applications which can be placed on a Web server and run by anyone with a compatible browser.

In this chapter we are going to learn about:

- HTML, HTTP and Java.
- Active forms.
- The Active Forms wizard.
- Running an Active form application within a browser.

Writing Web pages

If you have created your own web pages you will already have met HTML (HyperText Markup Language). This is the language used to specify not only the content of your Web page but also its appearance. You can specify the position, size and colour of text, how and where graphics are included - in short all of the aspects which make up a Web page. HTML has a series of tags which specify different aspects of the application, for example the first tag always indicates that the page is written in HTML, the same tag with a slash before it indicates the end of the page, for example:

> *<HTML>*
> *<TITLE> This title appears at the top of the page </TITLE>*
> *<H1> This is a header on the page </H1>*
> *</HTML>*

The same technique is used throughout HTML, a tag is specified, enclosed in angled brackets and terminated by the same tag, but with a slash in front of the key word. The terminating tag need not be on the same line.

If Web pages on a server are to be viewed by clients they need to have a unique address. The URL (Universal Resource Location) is a convention which specifies a unique address for every Web page. If you go to a particular location, such as the Borland pages : http//www.borland.com, the contents of the Web page are transferred to your browser where they will be interpreted and the Web page displayed. The page, which is likely to be in HTML, will be downloaded to your browser using HTTP.

Using Java

HTML allows you to write Web pages and to add HyperText links to other pages, to create the familiar browsing environment that we are familiar with, but the pages are still quite static. One of the most exciting new developments to help overcome this limitation has been the Java language. Java was originally developed by Sun Microsystems and is based on the C++ programming language. There are now some excellent Java development environments available, the most popular is Microsoft's Visual J++, but the new Borland environment JBuilder is more extensive. If you like Delphi, you will probably enjoy using JBuilder. Java has all of the facilities that you would expect of a modern object oriented programming language and extensive support from a set of standard packages (these are class libraries).

Java applications still need HTML to provide a shell around them and a new <JAVA> tag has been introduced into the latest versions of HTML to support this. The HTML page is executed until the <JAVA> tag is found. The Java application, or applet as it is more correctly called, then executes. When the applet finishes, the HTML page continues. There is considerable controversy about the use of Java. Java applets are down-loaded from the WWW server to your computer and then run using your computer's resources. Originally, for security reasons, Java was not intended to have any access to the file system of the computer on which it was running, but there was considerable demand for this and Java packages are widely available which allow you to do this. This can cause some serious problems. Some popular Web pages receive thousands of 'hits' per week. A page with a title such as 'Free Money!' will attract a lot of readers. If the page contains a virus written in Java, there is potentially a serious problem. As we will see later, your browser will warn you if you are reading a page with a Java applet or an Active Form, but you can easily override it.

The main benefit of Java is that you can write interactive Web applications which can be run across the WWW. The main problem is that you are more open to dangerous viruses. There is also a less serious problem with Java, in that you need a browser which is capable of understanding Java, in the same way as it is capable of understanding HTML. This is not as straightforward as it sounds, since Java is advancing at such a rapid rate. If you are using an old browser, you may find that you cannot run applets written in the latest versions of Java. Worst still, some manufacturers are developing their own versions of Java which are not fully compatible with each other. Since one of the greatest things about the WWW was that you could read pages irrespective of what computer or browser you were using, this is a serious problem.

ActiveX components

Delphi makes extensive use of components. The most familiar are the components with a visual interface, such as buttons. You can create ActiveX components within Delphi which may or may not have a visual interface. These components can be used within Delphi or within any environment which supports ActiveX. These environments include Visual Basic, Visual C++ and Web pages.

ActiveX components are a recent development of DLL (Dynamic Link Libraries), which allow you to write a reusable library of procedures in one language and to use them in another. ActiveX components, unlike DLLs, are object oriented and fit seamlessly into Delphi applications.

ActiveX and Java

ActiveX is an alternative technology to Java for writing interactive Web applications. An Active Form allows is a form based application which is treated as if it were an ActiveX component. The result of this is that when an HTML page is read, it can execute the Active Form within the browser environment. Virtually everything that you can do within Delphi you can do within an Active Form and run within your Web page. Delphi offers an Active Forms Wizard which greatly simplifies the process and even generates a simple HTML file which runs the Active Form within the browser.

The Active Form

To create and test the Active Form you will need a browser which supports ActiveX technology. Netscape Navigator 4.0 and Microsoft Explorer 3.0 support ActiveX. Explorer is used in this chapter. You do not need access to a Web server or even an active Internet connection to try out the examples.

The application produced is a drawing system, which is straightforward to develop in Delphi, more difficult to produce in Java and impossible in HTML. The running application within the browser environment is shown in fig 10.1.

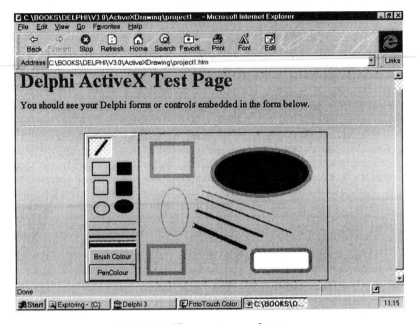

Fig 10.1 The running application.

Apart from using the Delphi environment and the Active Form Wizard, no additional code has had to be written to run this application within the browser.

Starting the application

To start the development:

- Select the **File | New** menu option.
- Select the **ActiveX** page.
- Select the **ActiveX Library** option.

All ActiveX Forms must exist within an ActiveX library. The next stage is to create a new Active Form:

- Select the **File | New** menu option.
- Select the **ActiveX** page.
- Select the **ActiveForm** option.

The Active Form Wizard is displayed as shown in fig 10.2, with the default entries.

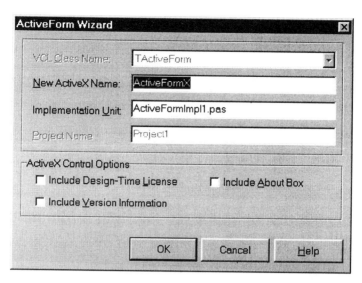

Fig 10.2 *The Active Form Wizard.*

The wizard supplies default names for the ActiveX name and the Implementation class, but you can change them if you wish. The Implementation unit contains the code which determines the behaviour of the Active Form.

What the application does

There are seven tools in this drawing application: line, rectangle, filled rectangle, ellipse, filled ellipse, round cornered rectangle and filled round cornered rectangle. You can also change the thickness of the lines and the colour of the **Pen** and **Brush**. The **Pen** is used to draw the outline of shapes, the **Brush** is the interior colour of the shape. The variable *Tool* is assigned to the tool currently in use. To add a shape to the form, press the left mouse button and drag. You will see a rectangle drawn with one corner fixed at the point where you pressed the mouse button, the opposite corner is at the current mouse position. This effect is called rubber-banding and is not automatic, some code must be written to implement it. When you select the button controlling the **Pen** or **Brush** colour, the Color Dialog is displayed.

Creating the User Interface

A **Panel** component provides the background for the tools. The tool controls are all speed buttons. The images representing what the tool does can be created easily using the Image Editor:

- Select the **Tools | Image Editor** menu option.
- Select the **File | New** option.

- Select the **Bitmap File** option. A file size of 32 x 32 is ideal for the tool images.
- Save the image to file using the **File | Save As** option.

You set the image on the face of the speed buttons by assigning the **Glyph** property.

The *Pen Color* and *Brush Color* buttons are command buttons. A Color Dialog must be added to the form for use by these two buttons.

When one tool is selected, it appears in a down position, when another tool is chosen this appears in the down position and the previously selected tool reverts to the up position, so you can easily see which is selected. Similarly when you have chosen a particular line thickness that button appears in the down position. This can be achieved without coding by assigning the **GroupIndex** property to be 1 for the tool buttons and 2 for the line thickness buttons. When a group of buttons have the same non-zero **GroupIndex** property only one can appear in the down position.

Your form should be similar to the one shown in fig 10.3.

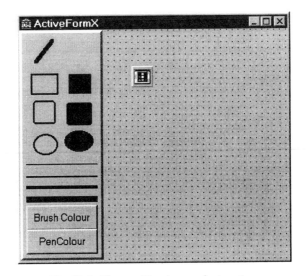

Fig 10.3 The application at design time.

This completes the design of the user interface. The more complex part is to write the Object Pascal code which drives it.

The Object Pascal code

All of this code is placed in the unit file just before the initialization procedure (the last procedure in the unit).

The type of tool is an enumerated type, declared in the **type** section of the application as *TTool*. A variable, *Tool*, of this type is declared in the **var** section. When a tool is selected by clicking on a button, the *Tool* variable is assigned the appropriate enumerated type. If the shape is solid the **Canvas.Brush.Style** property is assigned to **bsSolid**, if it is just an outline it is assigned to **bsClear**.

When the mouse button is pressed, the boolean variable *Enable* is assigned to True. If this variable is False, the mouse movements are ignored.

When the buttons to change the **Pen** and **Brush** colour are selected, the Color Dialog is displayed and the chosen colour assigned.

As the mouse is moved, a rectangle is drawn with one corner fixed and the other corner at the current mouse position. When the mouse is moved again, the previous rectangle is overwritten with a rectangle of the same colour as the background, effectively erasing it. A new rectangle is drawn.

The complete listing of the application is shown below.

```
type
TTool = (None, Line, Rectangle, Ellipse, RoundRect,
FilledRect, FilledRoundRect, FilledEllipse);
var
Tool : TTool;
Enable : Boolean;
StartX, StartY, PreviousX, PreviousY : Integer;

procedure TActiveFormX.SpeedButton1Click(Sender: TObject);
begin
     Tool := Line;
end;

procedure TActiveFormX.SpeedButton2Click(Sender: TObject);
begin
{Rectangle }
     Tool := Rectangle;
     Canvas.Brush.Style := bsClear;
end;

procedure TActiveFormX.SpeedButton3Click(Sender: TObject);
begin
{Ellipse}
     Tool := Ellipse;
     Canvas.Brush.Style := bsClear;
end;

procedure TActiveFormX.SpeedButton4Click(Sender: TObject);
{Rounded Rectangle }
begin
     Tool := RoundRect;
     Canvas.Brush.Style := bsClear;
end;
```

```
procedure TActiveFormX.SpeedButton5Click(Sender: TObject);
{FilledRect}
begin
    Tool := FilledRect;
    Canvas.Brush.Style := bsSolid;
end;

procedure TActiveFormX.SpeedButton6Click(Sender: TObject);
{Filled Ellipse}
begin
    Tool := FilledEllipse;
    Canvas.Brush.Style := bsSolid;
end;

procedure TActiveFormX.SpeedButton7Click(Sender: TObject);
begin
    Tool := FilledRoundRect;
    Canvas.Brush.Style := bsSolid;
end;

procedure TActiveFormX.FormMouseMove(Sender: TObject; Shift:
ShiftState;  X, Y: Integer);
begin
    if Enable = True then
    begin
        Canvas.Pen.Mode := pmNotXor;
        case Tool of
        Rectangle, FilledRect :
        begin
            Canvas.Rectangle(StartX, StartY, PreviousX, PreviousY);
            Canvas.Rectangle(StartX, StartY, X , Y);
        end;
        RoundRect, FilledRoundRect :
        begin
            Canvas.RoundRect(StartX,StartY,PreviousX,
PreviousY, 20, 20);
            Canvas.RoundRect(StartX,StartY,X,Y,20,20);
        end;
        Ellipse, FilledEllipse :
        begin
            Canvas.Ellipse(StartX, StartY, PreviousX, PreviousY);
            Canvas.Ellipse(StartX, StartY, X, Y);
        end;
        Line :
```

```
          begin
              Canvas.MoveTo(StartX, StartY);
              Canvas.LineTo(PreviousX, PreviousY);
              Canvas.Moveto(StartX, StartY);
              Canvas.LineTo(X, Y);
          end;
      end;
      PreviousX := X;
      PreviousY := Y;
      end;
Canvas.Pen.Mode := pmCopy;
end;


procedure TActiveFormX.FormMouseDown(Sender: TObject;
Button: MouseButton;  Shift: TShiftState; X, Y: Integer);
begin
StartX := X;
StartY := Y;
PreviousX := X;
PreviousY := Y;
Canvas.MoveTo(X, Y);
Enable := True;
end;


procedure TActiveFormX.FormMouseUp(Sender: TObject;
Button: MouseButton;  Shift: TShiftState; X, Y: Integer);
begin
Enable := False;
case Tool of
    Line : Canvas.LineTo(X, Y);
    Rectangle, FilledRect:Canvas.Rectangle(StartX, StartY, X, Y);
    RoundRect, FilledRoundRect : Canvas.RoundRect(StartX, StartY, X, Y,
20, 20);
    Ellipse, FilledEllipse : Canvas.Ellipse(StartX, StartY ,X ,Y);
    end;
end;


procedure TActiveFormX.FormCreate(Sender: TObject);
begin
Tool := None;
Enable := False;
end;


procedure TActiveFormX.Button1Click(Sender: TObject);
{assign the Pen colour}
```

```
begin
ColorDialog1.Execute;
Canvas.Pen.Color := ColorDialog1.Color;
end;

procedure TActiveFormX.Button2Click(Sender: TObject);
{assign the Brush colour}
begin
ColorDialog1.Execute;
Canvas.Brush.Color := ColorDialog1.Color;
end;

procedure TActiveFormX.SpeedButton8Click(Sender: TObject);
{give the pen a width of 1}
begin
Canvas.Pen.Width := 1;
end;

procedure TActiveFormX.SpeedButton9Click(Sender: TObject);
{give the pen a width of 2}
begin
Canvas.Pen.Width := 2;
end;

procedure TActiveFormX.SpeedButton10Click(Sender: TObject);
{give the pen a width of 4}
begin
Canvas.Pen.Width := 4;
end;

procedure TActiveFormX.SpeedButton12Click(Sender: TObject);
{give the pen a width of 8}
begin
Canvas.Pen.Width := 8;
end;

initialization
 ......
```

Web Deployment

When this application is compiled it produces an ActiveX OCX. To test your application in your Web browser select the **Project | Web Deployment Options**. This dialog is shown in fig 10.4.

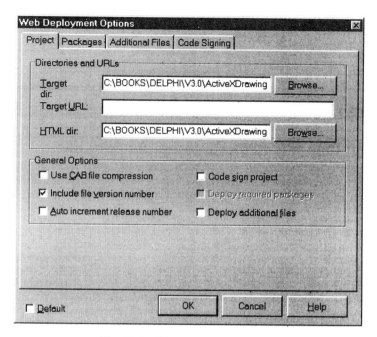

Fig 10.4 The Active Form wizard.

You need to specify the following three directories and URL:

- **Target dir**. This is the directory where the OCX file will be placed.
- **Target URL**. The URL directory corresponding to the target directory, for example if the URL for the target directory on your server was *http://www.mega.com* you would specify this here. At this stage if you do not have access to a server and want to test your application locally you can specify the target directory again rather than a URL.
- **HTML dir**. The directory where Delphi will place the HTML file which you can use to test the application.

CAB file compression will compress the OCX files if required. You do not need to specify any other option to test the application.

The Web page created

The **Web Deploy** menu option creates an HTML file which you can run from your browser. This file is shown below:

```
<HTML>
<H1> Delphi ActiveX Test Page </H1><P>
You should see your Delphi forms or controls embedded in the form below.
<HR><center><P>
<OBJECT
```

```
classid="clsid:7F0C246F-0CAE-11D1-8773-CBC70D5FE366"
codebase="c:/books/delphi/v3.0/activexdrawing/Project1.ocx
#version=1,0,0,0"
width=350
height=250
align=center
hspace=0
vspace=0
>
</OBJECT>
</HTML>
```

The page this produces can be seen in fig 10.1.

Running the application

To test out the application, run your web browser and specify the location of the HTML file. If you are using the default security settings in Explorer you will see the warning message shown in fig 10.5.

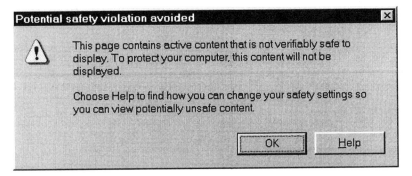

Fig 10.5 *Explorer warning message.*

You can solve this problem by selecting the **View | Options** menu and going to the **Security** page. In the section headed **Active content** make sure that the top three check boxes (and also the fourth if you are using Java) are checked as shown in fig 10.6.

Click on the **Safety Level** button shown in fig 10.6 and select the **Medium** security level. The application will now run, but the browser is likely to show a warning message asking if you are sure that you want to run an active application on your computer.

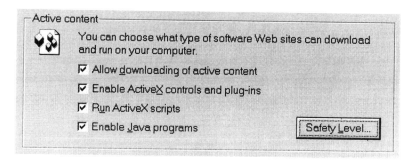

Fig 10.6 *Allowing ActiveX components and forms to be downloaded.*

If you find that the application runs but contains some bugs, you need to return to Delphi again, make the corrections and select the **Project | Web Deploy** option again. When you return to Explorer remember to refresh using the **View | Refresh** option. Since you may need to visit this application several times to get it working correctly it is a good idea to save its location as one of your "favourites" (in Explorer) or as a "bookmark" in Navigator.

11

Mouse and Keyboard Events

Introduction

In a Windows application, whenever you click on a button or move the mouse, keyboard and mouse events occur. Usually when you type text into an edit box, you do not explicitly want to respond to these events, you simply want Delphi to accept the characters and to display them. Sometimes you want to trap these characters and to take some special action. Similarly when you move the mouse a stream of events are occurring. Mouse and keyboard events are crucial to many Windows applications.

In this chapter you will learn about:

- The mouse events.
- Dragging and dropping components.
- The keyboard events.

The mouse events

The mouse events seem more intuitive to understand than the keyboard events, so we will look at these first. Whenever you click on any of the mouse buttons, two events occur:

- **OnMouseUp**.
- **OnMouseDown**.

Whenever you move the mouse many **OnMouseMove** events occur. The number that your Delphi application can respond to depends on how fast your computer is.

For all of these events, Delphi constructs the template event handler and passes five parameters:

Table 11.1 *The parameters of the mouse events.*

Parameter	Meaning
Sender	The object that detects the mouse event.
Button	Indicates if the left, right, or middle button was used, either *mbLeft*, *mbRight* or *mbMiddle*.
Shift	Gives the state of the **Alt**, **Ctrl** and **Shift** keys at the time of the event.
X	The X co-ordinate of the mouse position.
Y	The Y co-ordinate of the mouse position.

If you need to determine which button has been pressed check the value of the *Button* parameter.

Tracking mouse movement

Every time that you move the mouse an **OnMouseMove** event occurs, you can trace the movement of the mouse on the form by drawing a line between the previous position of the mouse and the current position. If you are using a dx4 or faster computer the line will appear continuous.

The running application is shown in fig 11.1.

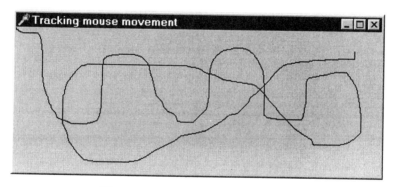

Fig 11.1 Tracking mouse movement.

To create this application start a new project and display the Events page of the Object Inspector. Double click on the **OnMouseMove** event and enter the following line of code:

> ***Canvas.LineTo(X, Y);***

The **LineTo** method draws a line from the previous position to the current position.

OnMouseDown and OnMouseUp events

The **OnMouseDown** and **OnMouseUp** events occur when a mouse button is pressed and released. A variation on the scribble program is to draw a line from the previous mouse position to a new mouse position when a mouse button is pressed.

The running application is shown in fig 11.2.

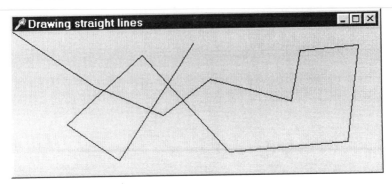

*Fig 11.2 Using the **OnMouseUp** and **OnMouseDown** events.*

To create this application, view the Events page of the Object Inspector and double click on the **OnMouseDown** event and enter the following line of code:

Canvas.LineTo(X, Y);

Dragging and dropping

One of the most common uses of mouse events is to handle dragging and dropping. In the next application, shown in fig 11.3, the right hand component can be moved by clicking a mouse button and moving the mouse while keeping the button depressed, that is by dragging. When the mouse button is released the image is drawn in a new position.

*Fig 11.3 Using the **OnMouseUp** and **OnMouseDown** events.*

Dragging and dropping requires co-operation between the component being dragged and the component which accepts it. To start dragging:

Go to the mouse down event handler for the image to be dragged (*Image2*) and add the single line of code shown:

*Image2.**BeginDrag**(False);*

This allows the component to accept mouse clicks without beginning a drag operation. The next stage is to get the form to accept the dragged component. When a component is dragged over another component or a form, an **OnDragOver** event occurs for that component. This has a variable parameter called *Accept*. If this is set to True, this component will accept a dragged object:

```
procedure TForm1.FormDragOver(Sender, Source: TObject;
X, Y: Integer;  State: TDragState; var Accept: Boolean);
begin
     Accept := True;
end;
```

The final stage is to specify how a dropped object is to be handled. You can do this in the **OnDragDrop** event handler for the accepting component (in this case the form).

```
procedure TForm1.FormDragDrop(Sender, Source: TObject;
X, Y: Integer);
begin
     Image2.Left := x;
     Image2.Top := y;
end;
```

In this example the **Left** and **Top** properties of the dragged image are assigned to the current position of the mouse.

There are a few further points to note about the drag and drop operations. If you try and drop *Image2* onto *Image1* nothing happens, since we have not prepared this component for accepting a dropped object. When you are dragging and move the mouse over this component the symbolic cursor changes to provide a visual indication that this area is not available for dropping.

Dragging to the right position

At first glance this application appears to drag and drop the component satisfactorily, but there are two problems:

- The dragged image may not move to the exact position you intended. If for example, you pressed the mouse button in the centre of the image, you would expect that when you moved the mouse and released the button that the same part of the image would be beneath the cursor, in fact the top left corner of the image is placed in this position.

- The image cannot be moved a few millimetres if the position that you try and drag the image to is within the current position of the image.

These two problems require some straightforward arithmetic calculations to solve them. When you press the mouse button to drag the component, you are supplied with two values, *X* and *Y*, which are the position of the mouse relative to the top left corner of the component. The position of this corner is given by the **Top** and **Left** properties. This is shown in fig 11.4.

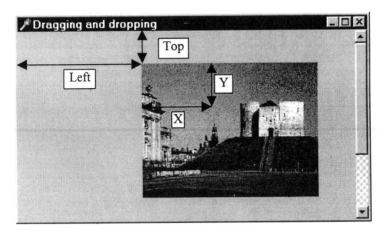

Fig 11.4 The mouse position relative to the component's top left corner.

The values of *X* and *Y* must be saved in the **OnMouseDown** event so that they can be used in the **OnDragDrop** event of the form to adjust the new position of the component.

Declare two integer identifiers *xShift* and *yShift* and assign them to *X* and *Y*, the current mouse position in the **OnMouseDown** event:

```
var
    xShift, yShift : integer;

procedure TForm1.Image2MouseDown(Sender: TObject; Button:
MouseButton; Shift: TShiftState; X, Y: integer);
begin
    xShift := X;
    yShift := Y;
    Image2.BeginDrag(False);
end;
```

The **OnDragDrop** event must be modified so that the new **Left** and **Top** values are adjusted by *xShift* and *yShift*, the position of the mouse when its button was pressed.

```
procedure TForm1.FormDragDrop(Sender, Source: TObject;
X, Y: Integer);
begin
```

```
        Image2.Left := X - xShift;
        Image2.Top := Y - yShift;
    end;
```

This code has solved the first problem. The code must be further amended so that *Image2*, in addition to being the dragged component, is also able to accept itself being dropped onto it. The code required is similar to that used for the form:

```
    procedure TForm1.Image2DragOver(Sender, Source: TObject;
    X, Y: Integer; State: TDragState; var Accept: Boolean);
    begin
        Accept := True;
    end;
```

The **OnDragDrop** event handler for the image must also be amended:

```
    procedure TForm1.Image2DragDrop(Sender, Source: TObject;
    X, Y: Integer);
    begin
        Image2.Left := Image2.Left + (X - xShift);
        Image2.Top := Image2.Top + (Y - yShift);
    end;
```

Note that the *X* and *Y* values supplied by this event handler are relative to the top left corner of the image and not the top left corner of the form, therefore the arithmetic required is different to that used in the **OnDragDrop** event handler for the form.

The keyboard events

Delphi has three keyboard events:

- **OnKeyDown.**
- **OnKeyPress.**
- **OnKeyUp.**

Every time that a key is pressed, the **OnKeyDown** and the **OnKeyUp** events are generated. However, the **OnKeyPress** event only occurs when a key that has a valid ASCII code is pressed. Alphanumeric characters, for example, produce the **OnKeyPress** event, but the keys with arrows, which are used for moving the cursor, do not. The sequence in which these events occur may not be exactly what you expect, for example, when **Shift+A** is pressed:

- **OnKeyDown** (Shift).
- **OnKeyDown** (Shift A).
- **OnKeyPress** (A).
- **OnKeyUp** (Shift A).
- **OnKeyUp.**

When a combination of keys are pressed, for example, **Shift+A**, or **Ctrl+C,** the **OnKeyDown** event passes the value of the previous key pressed down to the next **OnKeyDown** event, so that this event is aware that a pair of keys has been pressed.

The **OnKeyUp** event only has the value of the last key combination pressed.

The **OnKeyPress** event is not created by the **Ctrl** or **Shift** keys and in the example it responds to the pressing of the *'A'* key. An important distinction between these events is that while the **OnKeyPress** event differentiates between *'a'* and *'A'*, **OnKeyUp** and **OnKeyDown** are not aware of the difference between lowercase and uppercase letters.

If you want an event handler that responds to non ASCII characters such as Page Up and Insert, you need to use the **OnKeyUp** or **OnKeyDown** event handlers.

Using the OnKeyDown event

The next application displays an image in an **Image** component. When the up arrow key is pressed, the size of the image doubles, when the down arrow key is pressed, the image halves its size. The parameter *Key* indicates the key that has been pressed. The Delphi defined constants **VK_UP** and **VK_DOWN** are used to identify the up and down arrow keys (**VK_LEFT** and **VK_RIGHT** identify the other two arrow keys). The code is shown below:

```
procedure TForm1.FormKeyDown(Sender: TObject;
var Key: Word; Shift: TShiftState);
begin
if (Key = VK_UP) then
begin
    Image1.Width := Image1.Width * 2;
    Image1.Height := Image1.Height * 2;
end
else if (Key = VK_DOWN) and (Image1.Width >=2) and (Image1.Height
>=1)
then
begin
    Image1.Width := Image1.Width div 2;
    Image1.Height := Image1.Height div 2;
end;
```

There are small refinements which when added to the code ensure that when the **Height** or the **Width** properties are equal to 1, the image is not reduced in size any more. Integer division of 1 by 2 gives a zero size. When the component has a **Height** or **Width** property of zero, it will remain at zero however many times the up arrow is pressed.

The KeyPreview property

If you add components to the form in addition to the **Image** component, you will find that when the other components have the focus, such as the memo box shown in fig 11.5, the arrow keys are processed by the memo box and do not reach the **OnKeyDown** event handler for the form.

*Fig 11.5 The **KeyPreview** property.*

If you set the **KeyPreview** property of the form to True, it will always execute the **OnKeyDown** handler. In the application shown in fig 11.5, when you use the arrow keys to move around the memo, the correct action is taken, and the image also changes in size. You can see which component has the focus and take appropriate action if you have set this property to True.

12

Creating and Using Graphics

Introduction

If you have ever used a PC to run an old DOS based application, one of the most striking differences compared to a Windows application, is the lack of graphics. If images are used thoughtfully, the application will be visually more interesting and easier to use. Delphi has the tools to help you incorporate existing images into your application or to create your own.

In this chapter you will learn about:

- Incorporating existing images into your application.
- Creating new images.
- Using the graphics methods.

The graphics controls

If you want to add an existing graphic to your application, use the **Image** component on the Additional page of the Component Palette as shown in chapter 5. This supports all of the popular formats of graphical files.

The **Shape** control which is also on the Additional page, allows you to add a basic set of shapes, including circles, rectangles and rectangles with rounded corners. You can control the colour of the border and the interior of the shapes. This is also shown in chapter 5.

Creating Images

There are several ways in which you can create graphics for your application. You can use any of the powerful drawing applications, such as CorelDraw, or you can take photographs with a digital camera, or use a scanner to digitise an image which is only available on paper. Unless you are very skilful, it is very difficult to produce graphics, even fairly straightforward ones such as icons, that look as good as those which are commercially available. It is usually better to take an existing image and modify it, rather than creating a completely new one. Delphi provides a powerful image editor which allows you to do this. It is on the **Tools | Image Editor** menu option. The image editor is shown in fig 12.1.

To open an existing image choose the **File | New** menu option which will allow you to browse for the file you want.

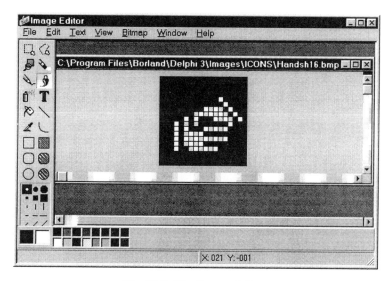

Fig 12.1 The Image Editor.

The image shown in fig 12.1 is an icon representing a handshake. Icon files are usually only 16 by 16 bits in size, but are surprisingly difficult to create so that they are visually attractive.

The Tools Palette

The Tools Palette on the left side of the Image Editor provides a useful set of tools for editing or creating an image. If you have used any Windows drawing applications, most of the tools will be familiar to you.

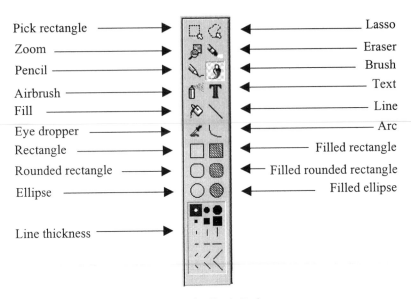

Pick rectangle ——————▶   ◀—————————— Lasso
Zoom ————————▶   ◀—————————— Eraser
Pencil ——————————▶   ◀—————————— Brush
Airbrush ——————————▶   ◀————————— Text
Fill ————————————▶   ◀————————— Line
Eye dropper ——————▶   ◀————————————— Arc
Rectangle ——————————▶   ◀————— Filled rectangle
Rounded rectangle ———▶   ◀— Filled rounded rectangle
Ellipse ——————————▶   ◀————— Filled ellipse

Line thickness ——————▶

Fig 12.2 *The Tools Palette.*

These function of these tools is shown in table 12.1:

Table 12.1 *The Tools Palette.*

Icon	Tool	Description
	Pick rectangle	Selects a rectangular area of the image
	Lasso	Allows you to draw a free-hand area which is selected.
	Zoom	Zooms into all or a part of the image
	Eraser	Erases parts of the image.
	Pencil	Draws a free-hand line.
	Brush	Paints free-hand.
	Airbrush	The longer the mouse pointer remains in one place, the more colour is "brushed" on.

	Text	Allows you to insert text.
	Fill	Fills an area which is one colour with another colour.
	Line	Paints a straight line.
	Eye dropper	Displays the colour under the mouse cursor.
	Arc	Draws an arc.
	Rectangle	Draws a rectangle.
	Filled rectangle	Draws a filled rectangle.
	Rounded rectangle	Draws a rectangle with rounded corners.
	Filled rounded rectangle	Draws a filled rectangle with rounded colours.
	Ellipse	Draws an ellipse (or a circle).
	Filled ellipse	Draws a filled ellipse.

Editing images

To start editing an image select the **File** menu and choose the **New** option to create a new image or **Open** to modify an existing image. If you select **New** you will be prompted for one of the three types of image files which the Image Editor can handle:

- Bitmap files (BMP)
- Cursor (CUR) files. These files are used to determine the type of cursor used. Forms, for example, have a cursor property which is assigned to a cursor file. Cursor files are always 32 × 32 pixels in size.
- Icon files. These are used to represent an application on your desktop. Icon files are small bitmapped images either 16 × 16, 32 × 16, 32 × 32 or 64 × 64. The Image Editor only supports 16 × 16 and 32 × 32 icons.

If you are working with an icon or cursor file, you will need to zoom in to see it more clearly. There are three ways of doing this, either by using the View menu options, the accelerator keys or the mouse, as shown in table 12.2:

Table 12.2 *Three ways of zooming.*

View menu	Accelerator	Mouse action
Zoom In	Ctrl + I	Double click.
Zoom Out	Ctrl + U	Shift + double-click.
Actual Size	Ctrl + A	None.

The best way to become familiar with the Image Editor is to experiment with it. Most of the functions are fairly straightforward, particularly if you have used any of the common Windows drawing applications.

Testing bitmaps, icons and cursors

If you are creating a new bit-map file select the **File | New** menu option and choose **Bitmap File**. The dialog shown in fig 12.3 is displayed. Most computers now have SVGA monitors which are capable of displaying images with 256 colours, but the default on this dialog is still VGA.

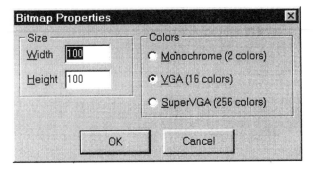

Fig 12.3 Creating a new bit-map file.

You can display this dialog at any time by selecting the **Bitmap | Image Properties** menu option which is only available if you are working with a BMP file.

If you are creating a new icon, you are prompted for the size of icon you wish to create and the number of colours available as shown in fig 12.4.

The most widely used icon today is the 32 × 32 icon with 16 colours. When you have created your icon, the **Icon | Text** menu option allows you to see what your icon looks like against a variety of differently coloured backgrounds.

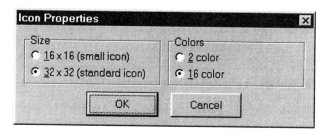

Fig 12.4 Creating a new icon file.

If you are creating a new cursor, you do not have to specify the size or range of colours. Cursors are always 32 × 32 pixels and have only two colours. To test your cursor, select the **Cursor | Test** option. If you select this option and drag the new cursor, the line is drawn from the 0, 0 position, that is the top left corner of the cursor. You can change this using the **Cursor | Set Hot Spot** menu option to be any position within the cursor.

When you have finished editing your bitmap, you need to save it using the **File** menu options **Save** or **Save As**.

Images, cursors and icons

To incorporate a bit-mapped image into your application, place an **Image** component on the form and assign the **Picture** property to the name of your bitmap.

You can change the cursor which is displayed when you move over a component (or form) by changing the **Cursor** property.

If you want the icon representing your application to be changed to the one you have created select the **Project | Options** menu option and view the Application page. Pressing the **Load Icon** button allows you to browse and specify your new icon.

Using Text

The way in which text is handled by the Image Editor has a few surprises. To add the text click on the **Text** icon. A vertical bar appears indicating the start position of the text. You can change this before you start typing by clicking the mouse.

When you type text it appears in the image. You can change the font of the text either before or while you are typing by selecting the **Text | Font** menu, which displays the familiar Font Dialog. You can also use the **Text** menu to change the alignment to left, centre or right relative to the position you clicked the mouse before typing. When you have finished typing and click on another part of the image or another tool you can no longer change the font of the text, since it is incorporated into the image as a pattern of bits.

Using Colour

The Image Editor allows you to choose:

- Foreground colours.
- Background colours.
- Transparent and inverted areas.

A typical Colour Palette is shown in fig 12.5. However it is different depending on the number of colours permitted in the image you are editing.

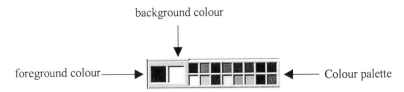

Fig 12.5 Selecting foreground and background colours.

To change the foreground colour, click on one of the colours in the palette. The selected colour will appear in the foreground colour box. To change the background colour, do the same with the right mouse button.

If you choose any of the drawing tools which require a mouse button to be pressed to draw (for example the pen), the foreground colour is the one which is used. If you do the same but use the right mouse button, the background colour is the one which appears. If you choose the eraser and use the left mouse button the background colour is applied, similarly the eraser combined with the right mouse button displays the foreground colour.

If you are creating an icon or cursor you can also specify transparent and inverted areas. These two options are added to the Colour Palette as shown in fig 12.6. They can be selected in the same way as any other colour.

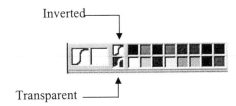

Fig 12.6 Selecting foreground and background colours.

The Transparent colour allows the desktop colour to show through. The inverted colour reverses the desktop colour. If you change the desktop colour, these colours change automatically. If you try and use these colours it seems as if the transparent colour does not work, however the background colour of icons and cursors when you start to draw them is the desktop colour, so anything you draw does not show up. To demonstrate this, start a new icon or cursor and change the whole of the image to be some other colour using the Fill control. Next select the inverted colour and draw one filled rectangle, select the transparent colour and add a second rectangle as shown in fig 12.7.

inverted colour

transparent colour

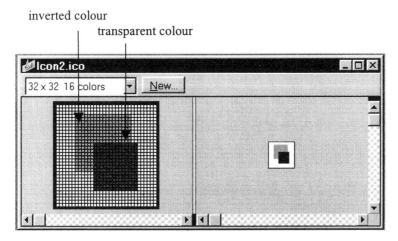

Fig 12.7 *Using transparent and inverted colours.*

Select the **Icon | Test** menu option and change the colour of the background. The transparent colour is always the colour of the background, while the inverse colour is the opposite of that colour.

Adding graphics at run-time

Most of the graphics you use will be images created or edited at design time using the Image Editor or another drawing package, however you can create your own graphics at run-time. When you draw graphics at run-time you draw onto the **Canvas** of an object. The **Canvas** is a property of the object and is in fact an object itself.

The four key properties of the **Canvas** object are:

- The **Pen** property, which is used for drawing lines.
- The **Brush** property, which is used for filling in shapes.
- The **Font** property, which describes the font of any text.
- The **Pixels** property which represents the graphical image.

The Pen property

The **Pen** property controls the appearance of lines that are drawn on the canvas. In particular you can control the following properties of the pen:

- **Color**. This is set using the RGB function, which specifies the individual red, green and blue components of the colour as values between 0 and 255.

- **Width**. The thickness of the line in pixels.
- **Style**. Determines if the line is solid, dotted or dashed.
- **Mode**. Specifies the way in which the pen colour is combined with the colour of the canvas which is being drawn on.

Drawing lines

To draw straight lines at run-time, use the **LineTo** method, which draws a line from the current point to the specified point. If you want to move the current point use the **MoveTo** method.

The top left of the area is the (0,0) position, and the default units are pixels.

In the application shown in fig 12.8 there are two sets of lines of increasing thickness from top to bottom.

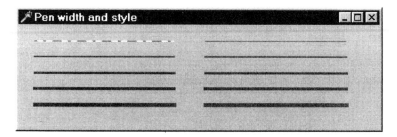

Fig 12.8 Pen width and style.

The left group of lines has a style of **psDashDot**, while the right group has a **psSolid** style. Only the first line in the left group is dashed. The dashed style is ignored for the other lines. This is not a fault with Delphi, most video drivers do not support dashed lines greater than one pixel in width. The code required to create this application is shown below.

```
procedure TForm1.FormPaint(Sender: TObject);
var
count: Integer;
begin
    Canvas.Pen.Color := RGB(120,120,200);
    for count := 1 to 5 do
    begin
        Canvas.Pen.Style := psDashDot;
        Canvas.Pen.Width := count;
        Canvas.Moveto(20, count*20);
        Canvas.LineTo(200, count*20);
        Canvas.Pen.Style := psSolid;
        Canvas.Moveto(240, count*20);
        Canvas.LineTo(420, count*20);
```

> *end;*
> *end;*

Note that the lines are drawn in the **OnFormPaint** event not in the **OnFormCreate** event.

The possible values for the **Style** property are **psSolid, psDash, psDot, psDashDot, psDashDotDot** and **psClear**.

You can draw directly on the form or alternatively you can create a **TImage** component and draw onto that using the **Canvas** properties of the image. If you want to draw a line directly onto a form, you specify:

> *Form1.Canvas.LineTo(200,400);* or *Canvas.LineTo(200,400);*

relying on defaults.

If you want to draw on an image called *Image1* you specify:

> *Image1.Canvas.LineTo(200,200);*

Ensure that the co-ordinates that you specify for the line are within the co-ordinate frame of the specified drawing area, in this case either the form or the **Image** component.

Drawing shapes

All of the shapes (and some others) that you can draw at design time can be drawn at run-time using a comprehensive set of methods. The most popular ones are shown in table 12.3.

Table 12.3 Methods for drawing at run-time.

Function	Action
Arc	Draws an arc - a section of an ellipse.
Chord	Draws the chord of an arc.
Ellipse	Draws an ellipse (or a circle).
FrameRect	Draws a frame around a rectangle.
Pie	Draws an arc and then draws lines to the centre.
Polygon	Draws a specified series of lines and joins the end of the last line to the start of the first.
Rectangle	Draws a rectangle.
RoundRect	Draws a rectangle with rounded corners.
PolyLine	Draws a specified series of lines but does close the shape.

The four parameters of the **Rectangle** method are the co-ordinates of the top left corner and the co-ordinates of the bottom right corner. The four parameters of the **Ellipse** method specify the dimensions of the smallest rectangle which will enclose the ellipse. The code shown below will produce the rectangle and ellipse shown in fig 12.9:

```
Canvas.Rectangle(20,20,300,120);
Canvas.Ellipse(20,20,300,120);
```

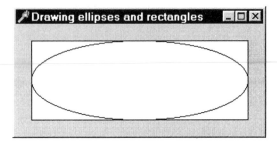

Fig 12.9 The Rectangle and Ellipse methods.

To draw a round cornered rectangle use the **RoundRect** method, and specify the same four initial parameters as for the **Rectangle** method and, in addition, a further parameter which specifies the diameter of the quadrant which goes into the corner of the shape, for example:

```
Canvas.RoundRect(40,40,300,120,50);
```

This code draws a round cornered rectangle of the same size and position as the previous rectangle but with a quarter circle of diameter 50 pixels in each corner.

The Brush property

While the **Pen** property of a canvas determines the size and style of lines, the **Brush** property determines the way in which areas are filled.

The **Brush** has three properties:

- **Color**.
- **Style**.
- **Bitmap**.

The **Color** property gives the colour of filled shapes and areas. You can change this at run-time by assigning the colour using the **RGB** function, for example:

```
procedure TForm1.FormPaint(Sender: TObject);
var
      c : Integer;
begin
for c := 1 to 255 div 5 do
      begin
{draw the top set of ellipses}
      Canvas.Pen.Color := RGB(0, 0, 0);
      Canvas.Brush.Color := RGB(c*5,c*5,c*5);
      Canvas.Ellipse(c*8 ,20,100 + c*8,120);
```

```
{draw the bottom set of ellipses}
    Canvas.Pen.Color := Canvas.Brush.Color;
    Canvas.Ellipse(c*8 ,20+ 120,100 + c*8,120+ 120);
    end;
end;
```

This produces the two sets of ellipses shown in fig 12.10.

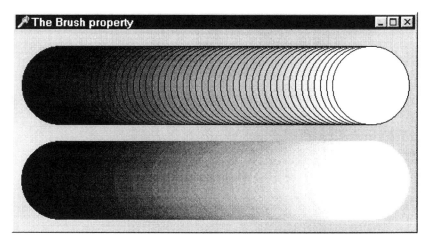

*Fig 12.10 The **Brush** and **Pen** properties.*

Note that in the bottom set of ellipses the colour of the **Pen** is assigned to be the same as the colour of the **Brush**, so black lines indicating the borders of individual ellipses do not appear.

The Style property

The **Style** property of the **Brush** determines if the brush fills the ellipse with either solid colour, or lines. The available options for the **Style** property are: **bsClear**, **bsHorizontal, bsVertical, bsFDiagonal, bsBDiagional, bsCross bsDiagCross** and **bsSolid**. Fig 12.11 shows all of these fill styles.

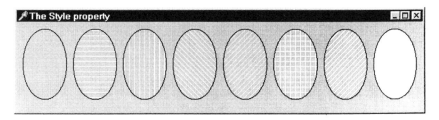

Fig 12.11 Fill styles.

The Pixels property

Any image is made up of a two dimensional grid of pixels. You can both read and set the colour of individual pixels. To read the colour you use the **Pixels** property of the canvas, for example:

*Form1.**Font.Text** := **Pixels[200,300]**;*

Changes the colour of the text on the form to the colour of the pixel at position 200,300. To set the colour of a pixel assign the **Pixels** property to a value.

***Canvas.Pixels[10,10]** := **RGB(20,30,200)**;*

The ColorDialog

An application often wants to be able to select a colour. You could do this by giving the red, green and blue components, but it is hard to visualise what colour this will produce. A better way of selecting colour is to use the colour dialog shown in fig 12.12.

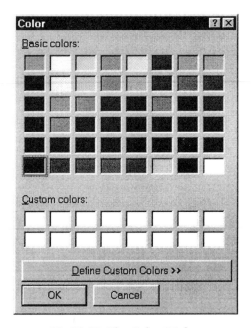

Fig 12.12 The Color Dialog.

The **ColorDialog** component is on the Dialogs page of the Component Palette. Add this component to your application, it does not matter where you place it, since it is invisible at run-time. To display the dialog use the **Execute** method:

*ColorDialog1.**Execute**;*

When you click on a colour to select it and then click on **OK**, the **Color** property of the **ColorDialog** component is assigned. To change the colour of the pen the following line must be added after the **Execute** method.

> *Form1.**Canvas.Pen.Color** := ColorDialog1.**Color**;*

Similarly the click event handler for the *Brush Colour* button is :

> *ColorDialog1.**Execute**;*
> *Form1.**Canvas.Brush.Color** := ColorDialog1.**Color**;*

The Color Dialog is discussed further in chapter 7.

Using the clipboard

The Windows Clipboard is a useful way of exchanging graphical information between applications. It is straightforward in Delphi both to read from the clipboard and to put images into it.

To copy information into the clipboard use the **Assign** method. For example, to copy the image in an **Image** component called *MyImage* to the clipboard:

> ***Clipboard.Assign(MyImage.Picture);***

If you want to paste an image from the clipboard into an image, firstly check that the content of the clipboard is a bitmap. The **HasFormat** method does this. This method is passed as a data type and it returns true if that type of data is held in the clipboard. To check for a bit-map image:

> ***If Clipboard.HasFormat(CF_BITMAP) then*** ......
> *{ if true is returned, the contents is a bitmap }*

A bit-map can be created using the **Create** method and the contents of the clipboard can then be copied to it:

> *MyBitmap := **TBitmap.Create**;*
> *MyImage.**Canvas.Draw**(0, 0, MyBitmap);*

If you want to delete *MyBitmap* after using it, you can do this with the **Free** method.

> *MyBitMap.**Free***

13

Menus

Introduction

Menus are an integral part of most Windows applications. Delphi has an excellent Menu Designer which streamlines the process of creating menus.

In this chapter you will learn about:

- Using the Menu Designer.
- Creating menus.
- Using the Menu Designer speed-menu.
- Using and creating menu templates.

Main menus and popup menus

Main menus appear along the top of a form, while speed-menus do not have a menu bar, but appear wherever the right mouse button is pressed. Both components are on the Standard page of the Component Palette as shown in fig 13.1.

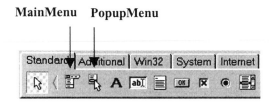

*Fig 13.1 The **MainMenu** and **PopupMenu** components.*

It does not matter where you place these components on a page, since they are invisible at run-time.

Both types of menus are created using the Menu Designer. To use the Menu Designer first place the menu component on the form. There are two ways of running the Menu Designer, either double click on the component or click on the **Items** property of the component in the Object Inspector. The design window is shown in fig 13.2.

Fig 13.2 The design menu.

The first item on the menu bar has the focus. The text you type will appear on the menu. Every item in a menu has its own set of properties and events. The text that appears on the menu is the **Caption** property of the menu entry. After you have made the first entry you can choose to enter another item for the menu bar or a sub-menu item.

Adding, inserting and deleting menu items

- To add a new menu item, run the menu designer, click on the position that you want the item to go to and type the text that you want displayed on the menu. This appears in the **Caption** property displayed in the Object Inspector. Next press **Enter**. When you have added an item to a menu, it is available in the form that you are designing.
- To insert a new item in the middle of a list, position the cursor on the menu item after the point where you want to place the new item, then press the right mouse button. Choose the **Insert** option from the speed-menu then continue as before.
- To delete a menu item, position the cursor on the item in the menu designer and press the **Delete** key.

Menu items can also be dragged by the mouse to change their position in the menu system.

Separator bars, accelerator and shortcut keys

Separator bars are useful for putting a line between items. They are menu items which have a hyphen as their **Caption**.

When you become proficient in using an application, you often want to use accelerator keys rather than using the menu; for example, to invoke the **Edit** menu on most applications you can type **Alt+E**. You can see in fig 13.3 that the **E** of the word **Edit** is underlined. In order for your application to do this, insert an ampersand (&)

character before the letter that you have chosen to be the accelerator key. It need not be the first letter.

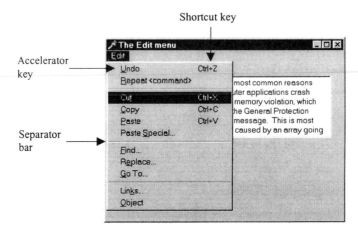

Fig 13.3 Separator bars, accelerator and shortcut keys.

Shortcut keys are similar to accelerator keys in that they allow you to choose a menu item from the keyboard. You can specify a shortcut key by setting the **Shortcut** property of the menu item to the key you have chosen in the Object Inspector. When you have chosen a shortcut key, this appears adjacent to the caption of this menu item when it is displayed. Delphi does not check for duplicates in either accelerator or shortcut keys - you need to do this yourself.

Creating sub-menus

Many menu items have sub-menus.

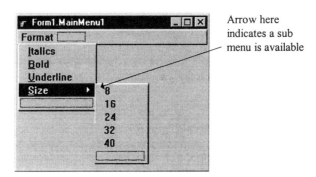

Fig 13.4 Creating sub-menus.

In fig 13.4 there is a list of menu options relating to the format of text, adjacent to the entry specifying **Size.** It is useful to have a further menu which provides a list of the available sizes, as shown in fig 13.4.

To create a nested menu, run the Menu Designer and position the cursor on the item that is to have the sub-menu and press **Ctrl→**. A small arrow head appears against this item. The items in the submenu are entered, amended and deleted in the same way as other menu items.

Designing popup menus

To create a popup menu, add a **PopupMenu** component to your form. Enter the menu designer in the same way by double-clicking on the component.

Fig 13.5 Creating a popup menu.

The Menu Designer as shown in fig 13.5 is virtually the same as when you are designing a main menu. The way in which items are inserted, amended and deleted is the same.

Popup menus appear when the right button of the mouse is clicked. In order for this to work, the **AutoPop** property needs to be set to True, this is the default. In addition you need to assign the **PopupMenu** property of the form which is to display the menu to the name of that popup menu. You can only have one popup menu per form.

The **Alignment** property of the popup menu is useful in controlling where the menu appears in relation to the position of the mouse when it is clicked.

*Table 13.1 The **Alignment** property.*

Value	Meaning
paLeft	Top left corner of the menu is placed at the mouse location.
paRight	Top right corner of the menu is placed at the mouse location.
paCenter	Top centre of the menu is placed at the mouse location.

Menu events

There is only one event for each of the menu items, this is the **OnClick** event. The name of the event handler is a composite of the form name, the caption property of the menu item and the event. For example, *TForm1.ItalicsClick* is the event handler for a menu item called *Italics* on *Form1*.

The best way of learning about a feature of Delphi is to try and develop a program using that feature. This section looks at developing an application for changing the style of text in a memo box using a menu and sub-menus.

- First create a new project and give the form a suitable caption - I have chosen *Changeling.*
- Create a memo box and set the **Lines** property to *Changeling,* or to any other text that you want.
- Add a **MainMenu** component to the form.
- Double click on the component and go to the menu design screen.
- The first menu header is *Format.* The menu items under *Format* are *Italics, Bold, Underline* and *Size.*
- The second menu header is *Colour* and has two items, *Memo colour* and *Font colour.* The *Memo colour* is the background colour of the memo box, while the *Font colour* is the colour of the letters in the box.

At this stage your menu design screen should be similar to the one shown in fig 13.6.

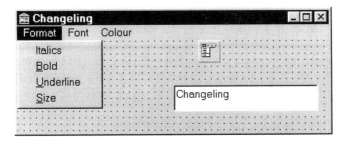

***Fig 13.6** The application so far.*

To add the sub-menu for the *Size* option, click the right mouse button over this option and press **Ctrl + →**. Type the possible font sizes as 8, 12, 16, 24, 32, 40.

If you return to your main form the menu is now in place - and you can run the program which has a complete menu system - the only drawback is that nothing yet happens to the text in the memo box. Some code needs to be written for this.

If you click on the *Italic* entry in the table in the design form you go to the template code for dealing with this event. To make the text italic you need to add one line of code to the event handler:

*Memo1.**Font.Style** := [fsItalic];*

However, you need to add more code if you want this menu item to toggle between italic and non italic. In addition you need to check to see if the text is bold. There are four possibilities to consider:

- If the text is italic, make it non italic.
- If the text is non italic, make it italic.
- If the text is italic and bold, make it italic only.
- If the text is non italic and bold, make it bold and italic.

The code for doing this looks like the code shown:

```
procedure TForm1.Italics1Click(Sender: TObject);
begin
                                {if text is italic make it non italic}
    if (Memo1.Font.Style = [fsItalic]) then
        Memo1.Font.Style := [ ]
else
                                {if not italic make italic}
    if (Memo1.Font.Style = [ ]) then
        Memo1.Font.Style := [fsItalic];

                        {if bold + italic make bold only}
if (Memo1.Font.Style = [fsBold, fsItalic]) then
    Memo1.Font.Style := [fsBold]
else
                        {if bold make bold + italic}
if (Memo1.Font.Style = [fsBold]) then
    Memo1.Font.Style := [fsBold, fsItalic];
end;
```

You need similar code in the event handler which deals with the *Bold* menu option.

All the code for dealing with the selection of a menu item is dealt with in the click event for that item, similarly there are click events for making the code bold or for underlining it.

You create the code for changing the size in the same way. Click on the menu item that you want to write the code for and you will go to the outline code that Delphi creates for you. The code that you need for changing the size of the text to 8 point is:

```
procedure TForm1.N81Click(Sender: TObject);
begin
    Memo1.Font.Size := 8;
end;
```

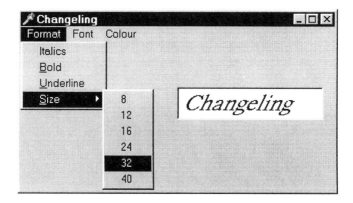

Fig 13.7 The running application.

You need similar code for changing the size to the other values. The running program should look like fig 13.7.

Changing the font and colour

If you want to change one aspect of the text at a time this is fine, but you often want to change several aspects, including the font, size and characteristics such as underlining and emboldening. Delphi provides an easy way of doing this using a common dialog box.

The **FontDialog** component is not only easy to use, but gives your applications a professional look. You need to include the **FontDialog** component in your design form. It is on the Dialogs page of the Component Palette. To display this dialog box you need to use the **Execute** method by putting a line of code in the event handler for the *Font* menu header:

```
procedure TForm1.Font1Click(Sender: TObject);
begin
    FontDialog1.Execute;
end;
```

When you run the program and click on **Font,** the font dialog box is displayed as shown in fig 13.8.

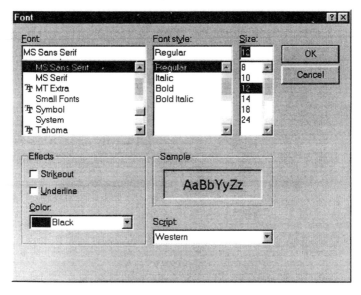

*Fig 13.8 The **FontDialog** component.*

You can change all the features of the text using this dialog box. To commit those changes to the memo box, a single statement is needed after the **Execute** statement:

> *Memo1.**Font** := FontDialog1.**Font**;*

The **Font** property contains all the sub-properties such as underlining, emboldening and size.

One minor problem with this dialog box is that a set of default characteristics is displayed, the font is **System**, the size is 10 and so on. If you want the dialog box to display the current characteristics of the memo box font, a bit more code is needed.

The whole event handler looks like this:

```
procedure TForm1.Font1Click(Sender: TObject);
begin
    Fontdialog1.Font := Memo1.Font;
    FontDialog1.Execute;
    Memo1.Font := FontDialog1.Font;
end;
```

The *Colour* menu option behaves in a similar way. Remember to add the **ColorDialog** component to the form.

The colour of the font and the memo background are changed by the code:

```
procedure TForm1.MemoColour1Click(Sender: TObject);
begin
    ColorDialog1.Execute;
    Memo1.Color := ColorDialog1.Color;
end;

procedure TForm1.TextColour1Click(Sender: TObject);
begin
    ColorDialog1.Execute;
    Memo1.Font.Color := ColorDialog1.Color;
end;
```

The Menu Designer speed-menu

The speed-menu displays the most common features of the Menu Designer. To display the speed bar, right click when the cursor is on the Menu Designer window. The speed-menu is shown in fig 13.9.

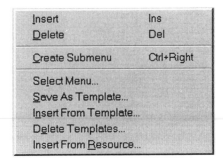

Fig 13.9 The Menu Designer speed-menu.

Menu templates

There are some standard templates available which deal with common aspects such as opening files. You can also create your own template menus.

If you want to use an existing menu template:

- Run the Menu Designer.
- Run the speed-menu for the designer by right clicking on the right mouse button while it is over the designer.
- Choose the **Insert From Template** option. The Insert template window is shown in fig 13.10.

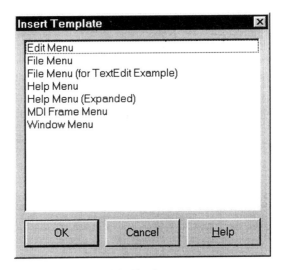

Fig 13.10 The Insert menu.

- Select the template that you want by either double clicking on it or by selecting it and pressing **Enter**.

If you want to delete a template choose the **Delete Templates** option from the speed-menu.

Creating menu templates

Any menu you create can be saved as a template. To save the menu:

- Click on the right mouse button over the Menu Designer to run the speed-menu.
- Choose the **Save As Template** option.
- The Save Template dialog box is displayed as shown in fig 13.11.

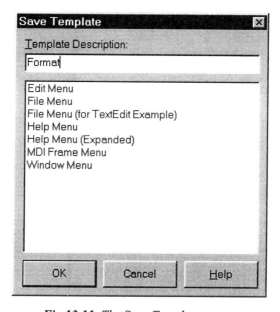

Fig 13.11 The Save Template menu.

- If you wish you can enter a brief description of the template in the *Template Description* section; this is just to help you remember what the template does.
- Click on **OK** to save the template.

14

Using Databases

Introduction

Many of the professional applications that are developed have large amounts of data stored in a database. One of the essential features of Delphi is that it contains the Borland database engine. This allows you to write applications which use databases to make your own databases and even includes a Database wizard which can greatly simplify the writing of a database application. If you want to have complete flexibility in how your application uses the database you can use a powerful set of data components which gives you complete control over how you use the database. One of the differences between versions 2 and 3 of Delphi is that database access has been speeded up. High speed coupled with a superb set of tools and wizards makes Delphi an excellent choice for developing serious professional database applications.

In this chapter you will learn:

- What databases are.
- How to create database applications using the Database wizard.
- How to use the data components.
- How to use the Database Desktop.

Relational data

The most common type of database, and the one supported by Delphi, is the relational model. In a relational database all of the information is stored in tables. An example is shown in fig 14.1. Every row in the table contains information on a single person, and constitutes a record. A record can contain many different types of data. Every grid entry in the table is a field. This does not seem very surprising, the real power of relational databases is the way in which information can be stored in more than one table.

First Name	Surname	Age	Department
Bill	Simmons	27	Finance
Jeanette	Damon	32	Marketing
Mark	Warden	47	Finance

Fig 14.1 *A relational database table*

If you wanted to retain details of the department which people work in, you could repeat the information for every person by adding additional columns, but this would cause a great duplication of data and would allow errors to creep in. If you wanted to save departmental information in this system you could add another table as shown in fig 14.2.

Department	Size	Location	Head of Dept
Finance	32	Third floor	Naomi Wilson
Marketing	12	Second floor	George Burford
R & D.	22	First floor	Ken Xia

Fig 14.2 *Reducing repetition of information with a second table.*

In the second table, the *Department* column is duplicated, but however many people are in a particular department the details only have to be stored once. This example has only two tables, but serious relational databases may have dozens of tables.

What databases can Delphi use

When you install Delphi, it is configured to allow access to the following databases:

- Paradox 7, 5.0 for Windows, 3.5, 4.0.
- Visual dBase, dBase for Windows, III+, IV.
- Access.
- FoxPro.
- Local InterBase Server.

If you want to use another database you need to install a driver specifically for that database.

Creating database applications fast

Developing applications which use databases is a very complex field which requires a good understanding of database models, client server architectures and a knowledge of the SQL (Structured Query Language). In this chapter we are going to look at three stages in database programming:

- Using the Data Forms Wizard to generate an application which uses one of the sample databases supplied with Delphi.
- Creating database tables using the Database Desktop.
- Using the data aware controls to write database applications.

Delphi supplies you with an excellent set of tools which greatly help you to develop applications in this area.

The Data Forms Wizard

To run the Data Forms Wizard select the **Database | Form Wizard** menu option. The form shown in fig 14.3 is displayed.

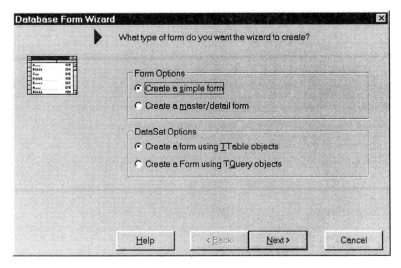

Fig 14.3 Starting the Data Form Wizard.

- In the Forms Options select **Create a simple form**.
- In the DataSet Options choose **Create a form using TTable objects**.
- Click on **Next**.

The form shown in fig 14.4 is displayed.

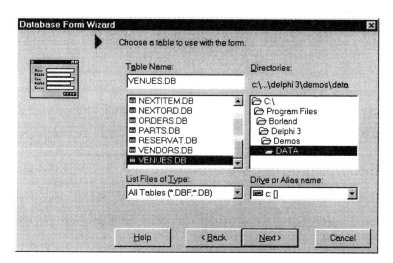

Fig 14.4 Selecting the database.

This form allows you to select a single table. In this example we are going to use the *Venues* table. If you have used the default file system when installing Delphi, this will be in the following folder on your computer: *C:\Program Files\Borland\Delphi 3\Demos\DATA*. Select this table and click **Next**. The form shown in fig 14.5 is displayed.

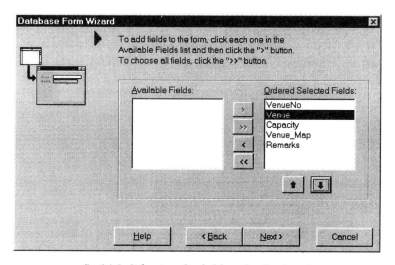

fig 14.5 Selecting the fields to be displayed.

When this form first appears, all of the fields in the table are displayed in the left list box.

- If you want a particular field to appear on the final table, select it and click on the right facing arrow.

- To move all fields click on the double arrow.
- To change the order in which the fields will appear, select the field and change its position by the vertical arrows.
- In this example, select all fields and click on **Next** to proceed to the next form. The table shown in fig 14.6 is displayed.

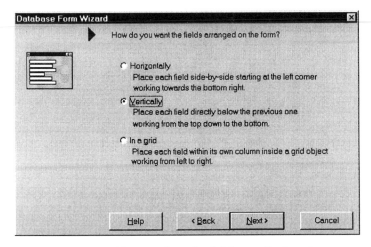

Fig 14.6 Choosing how the fields are displayed.

This form determines how the fields are displayed. The graphic on the left of the form shows how the completed form will look. In this example choose **Vertically**. Press the **Next** button to proceed. On the next form choose the **Left** option to display the labels on the left of the fields.

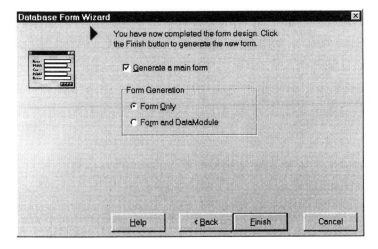

Fig 14.7 Generating a main form.

The final form is shown in fig 14.7.

Ensure that the **Generate a main form** check box is checked. This will ensure that when your application runs, the form produced by the Data Form Wizard is the first form displayed.

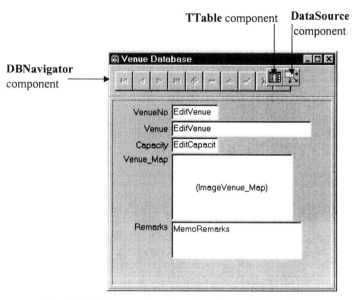

Fig 14.8 The completed application at design time.

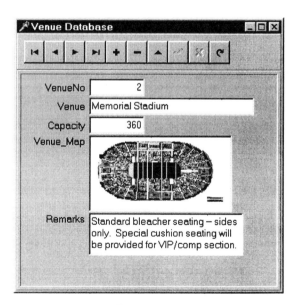

Fig 14.9 The running application.

The completed form produced is shown in fig 14.8.

You will recognise many of the features of this form, but there are a few components which you may not have seen before: the **Table**, **DataSource** and **DBNavigator** components. We will look at these in detail later in this chapter.

At run-time the **Table** and **DataSource** components are invisible. The **DBNavigator** component is used to move through the table.

The function of each part of the **DBNavigator** component is shown in table 14.1.

The running application is shown in fig 14.9.

*Table 14.1 The **DBNavigator** component.*

Icon	Action
⏮	Moves to the first record in the table.
◀	Moves to the previous record in the table.
▶	Moves to the next record in the table.
⏭	Moves to the last record in the table.
✚	Inserts a new record at the current position.
▬	Deletes the current record.
▲	Allows the current record to be edited.
✓	Writes changes in the current record to the database.
✗	Cancels any changes made to the current record.
↻	Refreshes the current record. This is useful if more than one user can make changes to the database.

The Database Forms Wizard is a powerful tool for viewing data, but its main limitations are that it can only view the data in a single table, and it only allows you to browse sequentially through the table.

The Database Desktop

If you want to create your own tables within Delphi you should use the Database Desktop, which helps you to create and modify Paradox, and dBase tables. The Database Desktop is a standalone utility which operates outside of the Delphi environment, but for all practical purposes it operates seamlessly with it. Unfortunately Borland do not supply any information on this tool in the Delphi manuals, simply a note to advise you to look at the on-line help.

Creating a new table

To create a new table:

- Select the **Tools | Database Desktop** menu option to run the Database Desktop.
- Select the **File | Open** option.
- Select the **Table** option.

The form shown in fig 14.10 is displayed.

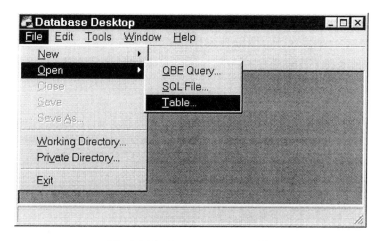

Fig 14.10 Creating a new table.

The Create Table form is displayed as shown in fig 14.11. You can choose the type of table that you want to create. Two types, MSACCESS and INTRBASE are not visible in this figure.

For this example choose the default type, Paradox 7.

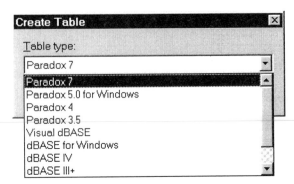

Fig 14.11 *Selecting the table type.*

The form shown in fig 14.12 is displayed and each of the required fields in the table must be entered. It has the following features:

- When choosing the **Type** you can right click to see all of the available options.

- For alphanumeric fields (indicated by a **Type** of A) the **Size** is the number of characters.

- If you want a field to be a key field, double click on the **Key** entry. A key field is indicated by a '*' in this column. There may be more than one key field but they must be the first fields in the table.

- You can specify the maximum and minimum values for numeric values. You will not be able to enter any data outside of this range.

- If you click the **Required** check box a value must be entered in every record for this field.

- The Picture edit box has nothing to do with graphics, instead it allows you to specify in more detail the format of a field. If you click on the **Assist** button, a list of possible formats is displayed and you can choose one. Examples include a string of letters with the first capitalised, and an unsigned digit. If the format you want is not available you can create your own. Look at the **Picture Assistance Dialog Box** in the on-line help for more details.

When you have specified the fields shown, click on the **Save As** button to save the table. Give the table a name of *NamesAndAddresses*. In the **Alias** text box, specify DBDEMOS. This will incorporate the table into this folder.

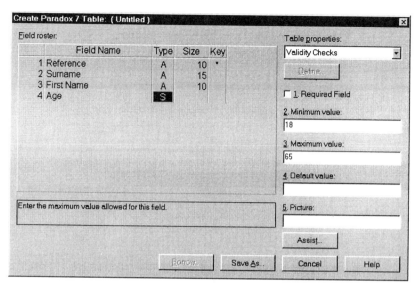

Fig 14.12 Specifying the fields.

Desktop tools

The toolbar on the Database Desktop is shown in fig 14.13. It has three sets of tools.

cutting and pasting   navigating the database   editing fields

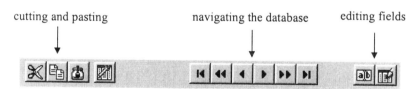

Fig 14.13 The Database Desktop toolbar.

- In the first set, the tools are used for cutting, copying and pasting. The fourth tool is used to restructure the current table. A dialog is displayed which allows you to control aspects of the fields, for example changing a field name or size.
- The first three navigation tools are used for moving backwards through the table: to the first record; the previous record set; and the previous record. The second group of three tools move forward through the table.
- In the final group, the first tool is **Field View**, which allows you to move through a field character by character editing it if you wish. The second tool **Edit Data** allows you to edit existing data or to enter new data.

Adding data to a new table

We have successfully created the table, but it still contains no data. To add data:

- Select the **File | Open | Table** option and specify the name of the table we have just created (*NamesAndAddresses* in this example).
- To add data select the **Table | Edit Data** menu option or click on the Edit Data tool.

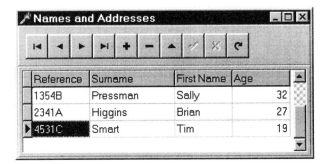

NamesAndAddresses	Reference	Surname	First Name	Age
1	1354B	Pressman	Sally	32
2	2341A	Higgins	Brian	27
3	4531C	Smart	Tim	19
4				

Fig 14.14 Adding to the table.

Fig 14.14 shows a few records which have been entered. When you have added as many records as you wish, close the form and leave the Database Desktop.

Reading the table

The table that we have just created can be read using an application created by the Data Forms Wizard. When you are prompted for the arrangement of fields specify **In a grid**. The working application is shown in fig 14.15.

Reference	Surname	First Name	Age
1354B	Pressman	Sally	32
2341A	Higgins	Brian	27
4531C	Smart	Tim	19

Fig 14.15 The running application.

Note that since the grid format was specified, several records can be seen in a tabular form.

Using data controls

The Database Forms Wizard provides a quick way of developing database applications, but sometimes you may want greater control over the way in which the data is transferred between your application and the database. Delphi provides a powerful set of components for doing this. These are on the Data Access and Data Controls pages of the Component Palette.

In order to write a database application we have to do the following actions:

- Make your application aware of the database it is connecting to, using the **TTable** component.
- Specify the data source, that is the database containing the data, using the **DataSource** component.
- Add data aware components to the form.
- Connect each component to a field in a table.
- Add the **DBNavigator** component.

We are going to look at each of these stages.

The Table component

The **Table** component is shown on the Data Access page of the Component Palette. Add this component to your application. It does not matter where, since it is invisible at run-time. The three key properties of this component are the **DataBaseName** and **TableName** and **Active**.

- The **DataBaseName** property in this case is DBDEMOS, which you can select from a drop down list.
- The **TableName** is the name of the table which we are going to reference. In this case it is **NamesAndAddresses**. This is also available from a drop down list.
- Set the **Active** property to True. This will ensure that the table is opened as soon as the application starts.

If you have not put your table into DBDEMOS, you can either specify the full path name of the file, or alternatively run the Database Desktop, open the table and press the **Restructure** icon. You can then choose the **Save As** option and save the table in this folder.

If you set the **ReadOnly** property to True, you will be able to view the data but not change it. The **Exclusive** property will ensure that only this application has access to the data.

The DataSource component

The **DataSource** component is also on the Data Access page of the Component Palette and is invisible at run-time.

The key property of this component is the **DataSet** property. This links the **Table** component to this component. Set its value to *Table1*, the default name of the **Table** component.

It may seem strange at this point that we need to have both the **Table** and the **DataSource** components, since the **DataSource** appears to do nothing apart from passing information from the **Table** component. The **Table** component is only one of a number of datasets which access database information, all of which need a **DataSource** component. The separation of the accessing of data from a database and making it available to the application is therefore split into two parts.

Data aware components

The application now knows what database and table are to be read. To display and modify the information read data aware controls are needed. These are on the Data Controls page of the Component Palette.

Many of these components are data aware versions of components on the Standard and Additional pages of the Component Palette. The component we are going to use is the **DBEdit** component. At design time this behaves in the same way as an **Edit** component. Add four of these components and appropriate labels to them, to display the information to be read from the *NamesAndAddresses* table. The form should be similar to fig 14.16.

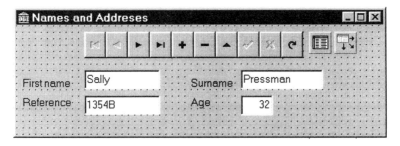

Fig 14.16 The application at design time.

Add the **DBNavigator** component which is on the Data Controls page of the Component Palette.

Each of the **DBEdit** components must be linked to the **DataSource** component and to a particular field. For each of the components, assign the **DataSource** property to *DataSource1*, the default name of the **DataSource** component. Assign the **DataField** property to the name of the appropriate field. You will be able to select from a list.

Finally set the **DataSource** property of the **DBNavigator** to *DataSource1*. The application is now ready to run.

15
Fixing bugs

Introduction

As the applications you write become more complicated, the errors will become harder to spot. Fortunately the new Code Insight feature of Delphi will help you write programs which are syntactically correct and there are a powerful set of tools to help you find bugs when they do occur. Everyone writes applications with bugs, rather more worrying is that even if your application contained no bugs whatsoever it would be impossible to prove it. Expensive professional applications from major software companies contain bugs (even Delphi!) although they have been extensively tested by teams of programmers. Bearing this situation in mind we are going to take a pragmatic look at debugging.

In this chapter you will learn how to:

- Use Code Insight.
- Use breakpoints to halt your program.
- Step through programs.
- View and modify data values at breakpoints.
- Trace programs.

Types of errors

There are three types of errors that you will come across when developing your applications:

- Syntax errors. The code you have written is not correct Object Pascal.
- Run-time errors. The application runs, but crashes.
- Logic errors. The application runs and does not crash but produces incorrect answers, or behaves in an unexpected way.

Syntax errors can be prevented and fixed by using the Code Insight feature of Delphi.

Run-time and Logic errors need the debugger to find out where the errors are and to fix them.

Code Insight

When you have finished writing your application you need to compile it so that you can run and test it. The Object Pascal language is formally specified in such a way that there can be no ambiguity, unlike a language such as English. The compiler checks that the code you have written is syntactically correct. If it is not then it cannot compile and run the program and will highlight the places where the errors have occurred so that you can fix them. If you have tried any of the examples so far, you will certainly have seen this in action. The Code Insight feature of Delphi helps to prevent you making these errors and can help you to fix them. This is a new feature of Delphi and really does make life easier.

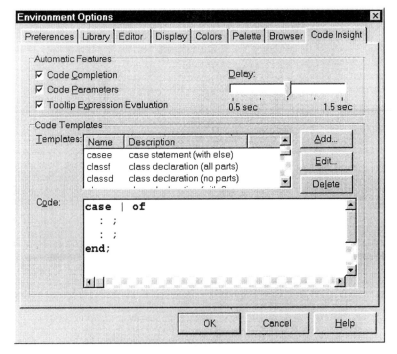

Fig 15.1 Enabling the Code Insight facility.

Code Insight monitors what you are typing and offers you possible valid options. For example, it will tell you the exact format of statements and offer a list of possible methods for an object. There are four distinct components to this feature:

- Code Completion.
- Code Parameter.
- Code Template.
- ToolTip Expression Evaluation.

To make sure that all of these are enabled, select the **Tools | Environment Options** menu option and display the Code Insight page as shown in fig 15.1. Check all three of the check boxes in the **Automatic Preferences** section.

The Code Completion dialog box is displayed when you have typed a class name. An example is shown in fig 15.2.

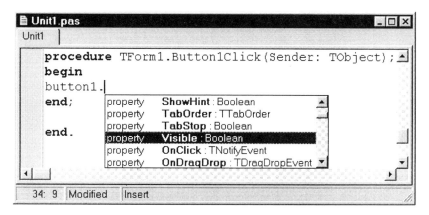

Fig 15.2 The Code Completion tool.

The more you type, the more the list reduces the possible options. To select an item in the list, either click on it and press the Return key or double click on the item.

When you are typing an assignment statement, typing **Ctrl+Spacebar** displays a list of valid arguments.

The Code Parameters tool displays a list of arguments for a method as shown in fig 15.3

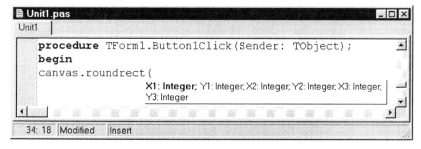

Fig 15.3 The Code Parameters tool.

This is an invaluable facility if you have used a method before, but are not exactly sure of the parameters. It does save a lot of time.

The Code Templates tool inserts commonly used programming constructions into your code. You can invoke this by pressing **Ctrl+j** at any time.

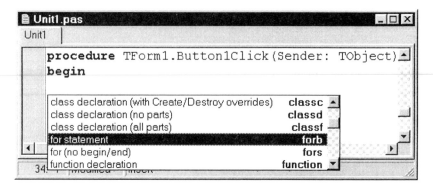

Fig 15.4 The Code Templates tool.

Fig 15.4 shows an example. The code inserted if this option is selected is an outline for loop with a begin end pair. You can add your own templates on the Code Insight page of the **Tools | Environment Options** menu option.

The ToolTip Expression Evaluation tool is of assistance when you are debugging. When you reach a breakpoint and move the cursor over a variable, its current value is displayed.

Run-time errors

If a run-time error occurs and your application crashes, Delphi will give you an indication of what the problem is and where the error happened, for example when an application attempts a division by zero as shown in fig 15.5.

One interesting feature of Delphi is apparent if you try to duplicate this error. You cannot simply put this line into your code:

> *Value := 1* ***div*** *0;*

Delphi will attempt to carry out this calculation at compile-time and flag an error at this point. If you make use of the code:

> *Solution := 1;*
> *Value := 0;*
> *Solution := Solution **div** Value;*

and do not use the values *Solution* and *Value* elsewhere, the optimisation of the compiler will reason that this code is redundant and exclude it from the application so that no error will be reported at run-time.

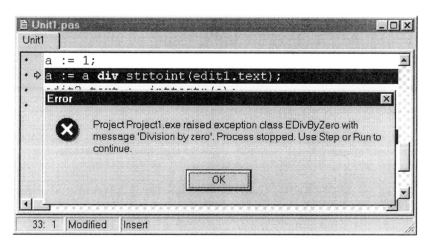

Fig 15.5 *Run-time errors.*

Logic errors

Logic errors are more complex to solve, since they do not cause the application to crash, but cause unexpected results. The debugger is extremely helpful in fixing these errors. The debugger has a range of powerful facilities, you can:

- Halt the program execution and look at the values of variables.
- Step through your code executing one line at a time.
- Make the program halt when a specified condition is met.

When you are debugging your application you need to tell Delphi to include debug information within the executable application. This will increase its size. Delphi is an optimising compiler and will look for ways of making the object code it produces as fast as possible. When you are debugging you will need to compile the application many times, so it is a good idea to switch off the optimisation. This will make the application run slower. When the application is fully debugged, you should compile without including the debug facility and use full optimisation, this will maximise the speed of the application and minimise its size. To do this select the **Project | Options** menu option and select the Compiler page as shown in fig 15.6.

Switch on all of the options in the **Debugging** and **Runtime Errors** sections and switch off the **Optimisation** option in the **Code Generation** section. When you have fully debugged your application, turn off the debugging and turn on the optimisation. For a full description of these options, use the Delphi Help. Display the Compiler page as shown in fig 15.6 and press **F1** and the context sensitive help will be displayed.

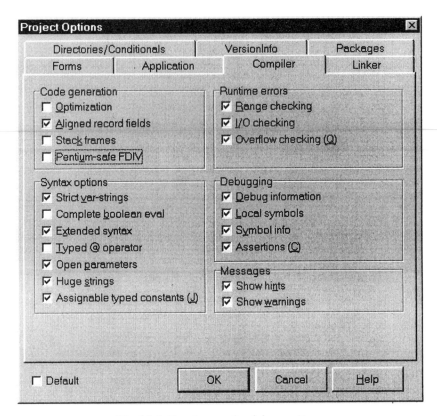

Fig 15.6 Turning on the debug options.

Stopping the application

The debugger allows you to run the program in the normal way until it reaches a point that you specify in the program. When the program halts at this point you can examine the value of identifiers and see if they are what you expect. You can specify the point at which your program stops in two ways:

- Select a line of code that the program will run to.
- Use breakpoints.

If there is only one point at which you wish the application to halt, you can specify this line in three ways, either:

- Click on the right mouse button, while the mouse is over the code editor window, to display the speed-menu and select the **Run to Cursor** option.
- Choose the **Run to Cursor** option from the **Run** menu.
- Press **F4**.

If you want the application to stop at more than one point you need to use breakpoints.

Using breakpoints

Breakpoints must be set on executable lines of code. If they are set on comments or other non-executable lines, they are never reached. Breakpoints can be set either before or at run-time.

To set a breakpoint, find the point in the code where you want the program to break and then you can do either of the following:

- Click on the bar on the left of a line in the code editor. The line will be highlighted.
- Bring up the speed-menu for the code editor and select **Toggle Breakpoint**.
- Press **F5**.

The breakpoints can be removed in the same way, since these commands toggle the breakpoint. There are other ways of setting and clearing breakpoints, but these three are the easiest.

Restarting after breakpoints

When the program execution has been suspended, and you want to restart it, select the **Run | Run** menu option or use the speed-menu. If you want to continue execution a line at a time use the **Run | Trace Into** or **Run | Step Over** options.

If you want to run the program again from the beginning choose the **Program Reset** option from the **Run** option.

Viewing breakpoints

If you have a large application with many breakpoints it can be difficult to keep a track of where they are. You can display a list by selecting the **View | Breakpoints** menu option. The window displayed and the code window at one of the breakpoints is shown in fig 15.7.

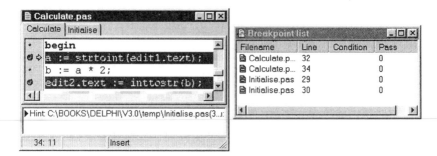

Fig 15.7 The breakpoint list.

The speed-menu for the breakpoint list is shown in fig 15.8. This contains some useful options.

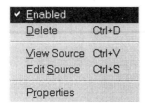

Fig 15.8 The breakpoint list speed-menu.

You can not only delete a breakpoint, you can temporarily disable it. You can also move directly to a breakpoint in the Code window by selecting either the **View Source** option or the **Edit Source** option. The **Properties** option allows you to change the characteristics of your breakpoints.

Stepping

Sometimes you may want to step through your code a line at a time. Fortunately you do not need to place a breakpoint on every line, you can use the step facility. There are three relevant options on the **Run** menu:

- **Trace To Next Source Line**. Successive lines of code are executed.
- **Trace Into**. When a procedure or function call is encountered, this option will allow you to follow the execution path into that routine.
- **Step Over**. When a procedure or function call is encountered this option will execute that routine and pause at the line after the call.

The Debug toolbar

The run and trace options on the **Run** menu are used so commonly that there are some icons on the toolbar that you should used as shown in table 15.1.

Table 15.1 *The Debug toolbar.*

Icon	Menu option	Shortcut key
▶	**Run | Run**	F9
	Run | Trace Into	F7
	Run | Step Over	F8
❙❙	**Run | Program Pause**	None.

Viewing data

When the program has stopped executing, you can examine data values in the program. The easiest way is to move the cursor in the Code window over the variable whose value you want to know. The ToolTip Expression Evaluation tool displays the current value in a small box.

If you want to know or modify the value of a variable, you need to position the cursor on the variable and select the **Evaluate/Modify** option from the debug speed-menu. The dialog displayed is shown in fig 15.9.

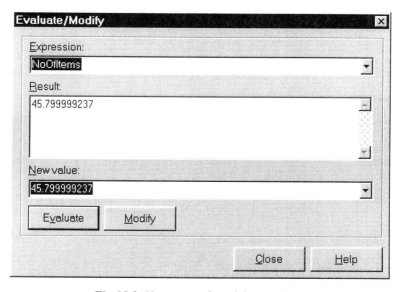

Fig 15.9 *Viewing and modifying values.*

If you change the current value of the variable, the application will continue using the new value.

Conditional breakpoints

Normally when you are using a breakpoint, you want the program to stop every time that it reaches it but, in some circumstances, you may want the breakpoint to be ignored. If for example you have a loop where the loop counter goes from 1 to 500, and you only want the program to stop when the loop counter reaches 500, you need to associate a condition with the breakpoint. When the condition is met the program will stop running at the breakpoint.

You set a conditional breakpoint by:

- Creating a breakpoint in the usual way.
- Select the **View** | **Breakpoint** menu option.
- Select the breakpoint you want from this list.
- Right click to display the speed-menu and select the **Properties** option to display the Edit breakpoint dialog as shown in fig 15.10.

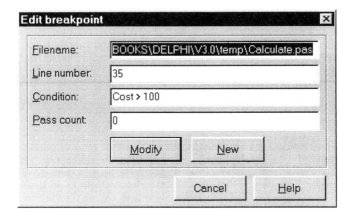

Fig 15.10 Setting conditional breakpoints.

In the condition edit box, set the condition you want. When the application runs, it will only break when this condition is met. Click on **Modify** when you have specified the condition.

Using watchpoints

If you want to monitor the value of a variable while the program is executing you can use a watchpoint. To set a watchpoint, move to the line where you want to place the watchpoint. There are three ways to insert the watch:

- Click the right mouse button to display the speed-menu and select the **Add Watch at Cursor** option.
- Select the **Run | Add Watch** menu option.
- Press the shortcut keys **Ctrl+F5.**

All of these display the Watch Properties window as shown in fig 15.11.

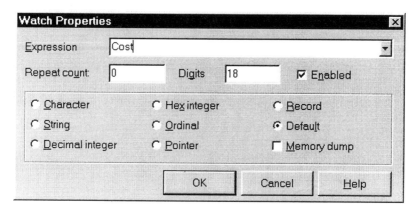

Fig 15.11 Setting watchpoints.

The expression you specify will be constantly updated in a Watch List window as the application executes. You are not limited to simply specifying variable names, you can specify expressions such as *Number * Cost*.

Pausing programs

If there is a logic error in your program and your program is looping endlessly, you may want to pause its execution. The **Run | Pause** command does this, or you can use the icon on the tool bar. You can later continue program execution in the same way as if a breakpoint had been reached.

If you decide that you want to end an application in an orderly way, choose the **Run | Program Reset** menu option.

16

The Visual Component Library

Introduction

Delphi contains a rich set of components on its Component Palette which are grouped by function into twelve sets in the Professional version:

- Standard.
- Additional.
- Win32.
- System.
- Internet.
- Data Access.
- Data Controls.
- QReport.
- Dialogs.
- Win 3.1.
- Samples.
- ActiveX.

Chapters 3, 4, 5 and 7 in particular look at the Standard, Additional and Dialogs pages. In this chapter we are going to look briefly at components on other pages which we have not seen yet.

The Samples and ActiveX pages are not described since these do not contain Borland supported components. The QReport page is also not described. In addition the Client/Server version of Delphi contains a Decision Cube page which is not described.

The Win32 page

These components are widely used and help you to create a Windows 95/NT feel to your applications. Some of the components are updated versions of the components found on the Win3.1 page. The components on this page should always be used in preference to those on that page.

TabControl
Representative of a notebook divider. This component allows you to add tabs to a form, each tab is mutually exclusive.

PageControl
A page set which can be used to make a multi-page dialog which can be changed by clicking on a tab.

ImageList
A non visual component which is a collection of images of the same size. Each image is referenced by an index. Double clicking on this component displays the Image List Editor.

RichEdit
In an **Edit** component all of the text is the same font, size and so on. This component allows text of varying formats.

TrackBar
A slider control that allows you to set a value between a specified minimum and maximum value by moving a tracker on a bar.

ProgressBar
A visual representation of the progress of some activity. This is an indication to a user of how long there is to wait.

UpDown
An up and down arrow, used to increment and decrement a value.

HotKey
Allows you to enter a **Ctrl/Shift/Alt** sequence from the keyboard which can subsequently be used as a hot-key to transfer control to another component.

Animate
Plays an AVI (Audio Video Interleaved) clip, which is a sequence of bitmaps. This is used throughout Windows 95, for example when emptying the Recycle Bin.

DateTimePicker
A list box for selecting date and time. You can type a new date or time or click on an arrow to display a month calender.

TreeView
Allows the display of objects in a hierarchical manner. The outline can be expanded and collapsed in a similar manner

		to the representation of folders in Windows Explorer.
	ListView	Displays a list in columns.
	HeaderControl	Displays a heading above a set of columns. Each column heading can behave like a command button to respond to click events.
	StatusBar	Creates a region for displaying the current status of operations in an application.
	ToolBar	Provides a container for tool buttons, arranges them in rows making automatic adjustments for their size and position.
	CoolBar	A container for a collection of Windows components which automatically arranges them in rows.

The System page

DDE and OLE are not covered in this book being largely replaced by ActiveX components, but Delphi still supports both.

	Timer	A non visual component which has an event which occurs after a time interval specified in milliseconds.
	PaintBox	Defines a rectangular area for painting.
	MediaPlayer	A VCR type interface for playing and recording multimedia video and sound files.
	OLEContainer	Creates an OLE (Object Linking and Embedding) client area for containing an OLE object.
	DdeClientConv	Establishes a client connection to a DDE server application.
	DdEClientItem	Specifies the DDE client data which is to be transferred during a DDE communication.
	DdeServerConv	Establishes a server connection to a DDE client application.
	DdEServerItem	Specifies the DDE server data which is to be transferred during a DDE communication.

The Internet page

These components speed up the writing of Internet applications. The full set are only available in the Client/server version of Delphi. Some cannot be used with access to a Web server.

All of these components are ActiveX components.

	FTP	This component is used for transferring files over the Internet.
	HTML	Displays HTML pages, with or without automatic network retrieval.
	HTTP	Implements the HTTP protocol client and allows retrieval of HTTP documents.
	NNTP	Allows applications to connect to Networking News Transfer protocol (NNTP) news servers.
	POP	Connects to POP3 servers for mail retrieval.
	SMTP	Allows connection to SMTP mail servers for sending Internet mail.
	TCP	Implements TCP for communication across the network for both client and server applications.
	UDP	Provides access to User Datagram Protocol (UDP) network services.

The Data Access page

These components provide a connection between an application and a database. Some are covered in chapter 14. All of these components are non-visual. The Client/Server version of Delphi has some additional components.

	DataSource	Connects a **Table**, **Query** or **StoredProc** component to data aware components.
	Table	Accesses data from a database and makes it available to data aware components through the **DataSource** component.
	Query	Executes SQL statements to access data from a database and make it available to data aware components.

	StoredProc	Allows access to procedures stored on an SQL server.
	Database	Makes a connection to a remote database server.
	Session	Provides global control over a set of **Database** components. Only required if creating a multi-threaded database application.
	BatchMove	Copies a table structure or its data from a server so that it can be modified locally and then updated on the server.
	UpdateSQL	Updates data on an SQL database.

Data Controls page

Most of the components on this page are data aware versions of components found on the Standard and Additional pages.

	DBGrid	A grid for displaying tabular information.
	DBNavigator	Navigation buttons that allow you to move through the records in a database.
	DBText	A data aware version of the **Label** component.
	DBEdit	A data aware version of the **Edit** component.
	DBMemo	A data aware version of the **Memo** component.
	DBImage	A data aware version of the **Image** component.
	DBListBox	A data aware version of the **ListBox** component.
	DBComboBox	A data aware version of the **ComboBox** component.
	DBCheckBox	A data aware version of the **CheckBox** component.

DBRadioGroup   A data aware version of the **RadioGroup** component.

DBLookupListBox   A data aware version of the lookup **ListBox** component.

DBLookupComboBox   A data aware version of the lookup **ComboBox** component.

DBRichEdit   A data aware version of the **RichEdit** component.

DBCtrlGrid   A data aware grid. Unlike the **DBGrid** component which displays each record in a single row, this component allows free-form layout of every record.

DBChart   A data aware version of the **Chart** component.

The Dialogs page

These dialogs are extensively used in virtually all Windows applications to provide a professional appearance. They are non visual, but when their **Execute** method is used they each display a dialog box.

Some of these components are reviewed in chapter 7.

OpenDialog   Displays the File Open dialog.

SaveDialog   Displays the File Save dialog.

OpenPictureDialog   Displays the Open Picture dialog.

SavePictureDialog   Displays the Save Picture dialog.

FontDialog   Displays the Font dialog.

ColorDialog   Displays the Color dialog.

PrintDialog   Displays the Print dialog.

	PrinterSetupDialog	Displays the Printer Setup dialog.
	FindDialog	Displays the Find dialog.
	ReplaceDialog	Displays the Replace dialog.

The Win 3.1 page

These components have been preserved for backwards compatibility with earlier Windows 3.1 applications. Most have now been replaced with other components as shown in table 16.1.

Table 16.1 Replacements for the Win3.1 components.

Win 3.1	Replace with	New page
DBLookupList	DBLookupListBox	Data
DBLookupCombo	DBLookupComboBox	Data
TabSet	TabControl	Win32
Outline	TreeView	Win32
Header	HeaderControl	Win32
NoteBook	PageControl	Win32
TabbedNoteBook	PageControl	Win32

These components should not be used in new applications, since there is no guarantee that they will be supported in future releases.

	DBLookupList	A data aware list box that displays a list of items using a lookup field, in a list box.
	DBLookupCombo	A data aware combo box that displays a list of items using a lookup field, in a combo box.
	TabSet	Creates notebook-like tabs. This component should be used with the Notebook component to allow different pages to be viewed.
	Outline	Displays data in a hierarchical tree-like format.
	TabbedNotebook	A multi-page component with several pages each with its own components, selected by clicking on a tab.

	Notebook	A multiple page component which should be used with the **TabSet** component to allow different pages to be viewed.
	Header	Provides a set of column headers which can be resized at run-time.
	FileListBox	Displays a list of the files in the current folder.
	DirectoryListBox	Displays a list of folders (or directories in Windows 3.1 terminology) on the current disk drive.
	DriveComboBox	Displays a list of the available drives.
	FilterComboBox	A filter to restrict the types of files which are displayed.

Index